G000150372

JUSTIFIABLE HOMICIDE

DAN BROWN

ISBN 978-1-63885-280-3 (Paperback)
ISBN 978-1-63885-281-0 (Digital)

Covenant Books, Inc.
11661 Hwy 707
Murrells Inlet, SC 29576
www.covenantbooks.com

CONTENTS

Introduction..5

The Mistress from Hell: Texas v. Frances Hall (2013) 7
The South Carolina Killer: South Carolina v. Debra
    Sheridan (2017) 18
Killing a Child Molester: Washington v. Yvonne Wanrow (1972)....23
Murder in Alabama: Alabama v. Jacqueline Dixon (2018)..............29
The Pine Street Shootout!: Oklahoma v. Erin Dukes (1997)...........33
The Death of a Terrorist: Maine v. Amber Cummings (2009)........39
A Deadly Confrontation: Virginia v. Breanna Sullivan (2018)........48
The Death of an Ex-Husband: Florida v. Cara Ryan (2015) 54
Deadly Dispute: Missouri v. Ashley Hunter (2015)........................65
Who Killed Jon Garner: Texas v. Sandra Garner (2018)..................71
The Cop Killer: New York v. Barbara Sheehan (2008)....................79
A Deadly Crash: Connecticut v. Cherelle Baldwin (2013) 87
The Dead Boyfriend: Florida v. Stacy Sabo (2018) 93
The Murder of Matt Winkler: Tennessee v. Mary Winkler..............98
The Millionaire Killer: Virginia v. Susan Cummings (1997)..........106
The Husband from Hell: Texas v. Charlene Hill (2006)..................114
The Case of the Burning Bed: Michigan v. Francine
    Hughes (1977)..122
The Death of an Oil Tycoon: Oklahoma v. Donna Bechtel
    (1984) 131
The Singer and the Skier: Colorado v. Claudine Longet (1976) 139
Two Birds with One Blast: Texas v. Tracy Roberson (2007)..........147
Final Analysis: Women Who Kill..155

Bibliography..159

INTRODUCTION

Twenty men have been killed in fifteen different states in the United States in recent years. In most of those cases, the victim was acquainted with the killer. What did each of these twenty cases have "in common"? In each case, the killer was identified as a "woman"! Each woman, after being arrested by law enforcement authorities, was prosecuted for criminal homicide with charges ranging from first-degree murder to second-degree manslaughter. How has the American judicial system treated a woman who is charged with killing a man? Is there "equal justice" in America? Under the Sixth Amendment of the United States Constitution, each person charged with a "felony crime" is entitled a trial by a jury composed of citizens living in the community where the crime occurred. This basic right raised another issue? Who serves on a criminal court jury in these types of felony cases?

Under the original Constitution, the determination of who was eligible to serve on a jury was left up to each state under the Tenth Amendment to the Constitution. During the 1800s and early 1900s, most states restricted jury service to eligible voters. However, from 1790 to 1920, women were *not* allowed to vote in America. Finally, with the passage of the Nineteenth Amendment (1920), women were given the right to vote and were, therefore, allowed to serve on a criminal court jury. Within the last few years, women have gained positions in government, serving as prosecutors and judges. What impact has women had on the judicial system since they have been allowed to serve as prosecutors, judges, and members of a jury? Are women in modern American being given the basic rights of "equal protection" and "due process of law" as guaranteed under the Fourteenth Amendment of the American Constitution? An examination of the twenty cases herein reveals some surprising results!

THE MISTRESS FROM HELL
Texas v. Frances Hall (2013)

Frances Hall was born in the 1960s during the turbulent years of the national civil rights movement. While in high school, Frances met a nice-looking young man, Bill T. Hall.

Frances knew that it was "love at first sight." They dated for the final two years of high school and made a commitment to get married as soon as they graduated. Frances and Bill got married in 1984. Bill was an energetic young man who worked two jobs during the early years of their marriage. Frances and Bill were blessed with the birth of their first child, a daughter whom they named Nikki, born in 1985. Three years later, the couple was blessed with a second child, an adorable young boy whom they named Jason. Frances was a stay-at-home mom during the early years of their marriage. In 1989, Bill and Frances decided to go into business for themselves: the trucking business. Bill bought his first truck-delivering products for several national stores. Francis served as the secretary, bookkeeper, and manager. During the 1990s, their trucking business expanded into a fleet of more than fifty trucks with over a hundred employees. The Bill Hall Trucking Company was a very successful business that generated more than $50,000,000 per year. Bill began spending more time from home as the business expanded into several states outside of Texas. While Frances continued to be a stay-at-home mom as their children finished their public education and eventually getting married, Bill was considered a "wild man" who enjoyed fast cars, motorcycles, nightclubs, and lots of partying! The couple gradually drifted apart with Bill enjoying the company of several young women during his road trips on behalf of his growing trucking company.

Bonnie Contreras was born in the mid-1980s. After finishing school, Bonnie wanted to further her education. Being from a poor family, Bonnie could not afford to go to college. Bonnie took a job in the restaurant industry waiting on tables and depending on customer tips to cover her living expenses. Bonnie shared an apartment with another young lady who worked as a waitress at the same restaurant. Realizing that making a living as a waitress was not giving her sufficient income to live on, Bonnie transferred to a more lucrative occupation, becoming an "exotic dancer" at a gentlemen's club. The pay was good, and the tips were outstanding! Some weeks, Bonnie was bringing home more than $500 per week. Bonnie soon moved into her own apartment in a nice complex designated as "adults only!" Bonnie would work during the late afternoon and evening hours from 4:00 p.m. until the club closed at 1:00 a.m. every day except Sunday. During a break from her job one weekend, Bonnie went to a local "spinach fair," agreeing to help her aunt in one of the food booths located at the fair. During that Sunday afternoon, she met Bill Hall when he came by the booth to buy some food. Bonnie was impressed by his pleasant smile and nice clothes. Bonnie wondered if he was "married." Bonnie looked at the ring finger on his left hand. No wedding ring! Maybe he was a single man looking for a nice-looking young lady. Her! After a few minutes of pleasant conversation, he asked for her phone number! Bonnie, without hesitation, gave it to him! A few days later, Bill called her and asked her out to dinner. Bill took Bonnie to an expensive steak house. Avery enjoyable evening! Bonnie invited Bill to come by the club where she worked to see her perform. Bonnie's performance blew Bill away! Bill and Bonnie started dating on a regular basis, seeing each other two to three times a month. During their courtship, Bill told Bonnie that he was going through a painful divorce and that she should be patient until he got rid of his old lady!

The Boiling Point (October 9, 2013)

Bonnie and Bill had been seeing each other for almost three years. Bonnie was treated like the queen of England during their courtship. Bill paid for Bonnie to have plastic surgery to enhance her appearance (breast implants). Bill bought Bonnie an expensive sports car! Bill took Bonnie on trips to Las Vegas! The ultimate gift: Bill gave Bonnie a *five-carat diamond ring* that was valued at more than $25,000! Despite all these gifts, Bonnie wanted Bill to finalize his divorce from Frances so that they could enjoy life together. While Bill was in the shower one day at her place, Bonnie went through Bill's cellphone and found the phone number for Frances! A few days later, Bonnie sent Frances a text, telling Frances that she was Bill's girlfriend and Frances should just give Bill his freedom so that he could get a divorce. The two women texted back and forth for several weeks. One day, Bonnie sent Frances some pictures of herself, naked in bed with Bill. This text blew the lid off the marriage between Bill and Frances. When Bill came home that evening, Frances confronted Bill about his relationship with Bonnie. At first, Bill denied the allegations. Francis pulled out her cellphone and showed Bill all of the pictures that Bonnie had sent her earlier that day. Realizing that he was caught, Bill broke down and confessed to the relationship, acknowledging that it had been going on for several months.

Bill promised to stop seeing Bonnie if Frances would forgive him and give him one more chance! Frances reluctantly agreed! Bill and Frances retired for the evening. The next morning, Frances awoke and saw Bill in the bathroom getting ready to go to work. Grabbing his cellphone, she saw where Bonnie had sent Bill several "nude selfies" telling him that she was ready to give him a *hot lunch*! Francis confronted Bill about the photos and decided to throw him out of the house, saying, "It is over!"

The Day of the Murder (October 10, 2013)

Frances Hall was totally distraught during the afternoon and evening hours of October 9, 2013. After having several glasses of wine, Frances was able to relax and get some rest. The next morning, the phone rang. Frances answered, hoping that maybe it was Bill! The phone call was not from Bill but an employee at the trucking company, wanting Bonnie to come down and sign off on several work orders and check the incoming mail. Realizing that several large checks were due in the mail, Frances showered, got dressed, and headed down to the trucking company offices. While driving along Texas State Highway 1604, Frances noticed that a black Range Rover wagon was approaching her in the oncoming lane of traffic. Getting closer, Francis recognized that the Range Rover was the one that Bill had bought a few months earlier, and it was being driven by a young woman with dark-colored hair. Several hundred yards behind the Range Rover was her husband, Bill, riding on his new Harley motorcycle. Frances was shocked! Who was driving her Range Rover? Why was Bill following behind the Range Rover on his motorcycle? Frances slowed down her Cadillac Escalade and turned her vehicle around, trying to follow the two vehicles. Speeding up, Frances was able to catch up with the two vehicles within three miles. Frances accelerated and passed the motorcycle and pulled in behind the Range Rover. Frances could clearly see that the driver was a young woman with long black hair. Frances knew immediately that the driver was Bonnie Contreras, the little "bitch" that had been tormenting her for the last several months with those "awful text messages"! Frances accelerated and started ramming the Range Rover with the front of her big Cadillac Escalade! One bump! *Bam!* A second bump, *bam!* Suddenly, Frances felt something crash into the back of her Escalade! *Bam!*

The Murder of Bill Hall (October 10, 2013)

Frances continued speeding down state highway 1604, without realizing that Bill had wrecked his motorcycle when she bumped the Range Rover that Bonnie Contreras was driving. Frances rammed the back of Bonnie's vehicle two more times, trying to force Bonnie to lose control and wreck the Range Rover. *Bam! Bam!* Bonnie accelerated her vehicle, going over a hundred miles per hour. Frances glanced into the rearview mirror and noticed that Bill was no longer behind her. Frances also realized that the back window of her Cadillac Escalade was knocked out. Frances slowed down, wondering what had happened to Bill. Had Bill wrecked his motorcycle during the car chase down the roadway? Frances pulled off the side of the highway and stopped her Escalade. Frances decided to call her daughter, Nikki, and see if she had heard from her father. Nikki answered immediately and told her mother that she had not talked to her father since yesterday. Frances decided to turn around and go back up highway 1604, retracing her steps. Frances started looking along both sides of the roadway to see if she could find Bill. It was getting dark and difficult to see the areas along the state highway. Frances saw no sign of Bill or his cycle along the roadway. Frances retraced her path all the way back up to the yard of the trucking company. No sign of Bill. Frances called Nikki again.

Still no word from Bill. Frances turned her vehicle around and headed back south on highway 1604. After about fifteen miles down the road, she came upon emergency vehicles and Texas Ranger's vehicle on one side of the road. Frances also saw the black Range Rover parked along the side of the road.

Oh my god, Frances thought! Where was Bill? Pulling up behind the emergency vehicles, Frances jumped out of her Cadillac Escalade and headed up to the scene of the wreck. She saw Bill's cycle lying down in a ditch along the road. Frances realized at that moment that Bill was injured or dead!

The Law Enforcement Investigation

Frances hurried up to see Bill. Law enforcement officers stopped her. Someone yelled, "That his wife! Let her through!" Frances rushed down to Bill's side as the ambulance attendants were loading him onto a stretcher for transport to the hospital. Bill's last words: "Baby, I am so sorry!" The attendants loaded him into the ambulance and headed out, taking him to the hospital. Frances cried, "Wait for me!" An officer grabbed Frances and told her that she would have to go and have a seat in a law enforcement vehicle. Frances did not want to go! She resisted. The officer placed the handcuffs on her and escorted her to the back of a sheriff's car. While being dragged to the vehicle, Frances noticed that Bonnie was being questioned by another sheriff's deputy. Frances tried to get to Bonnie. The sheriff's deputy pulled her away and forcibly placed her in the back of his unit. Frances was questioned for several minutes but refused to answer questions after being given her Miranda rights warning. Frances was taken to the Bexar county jail. Frances was told that Bill had died on the way to the hospital. Frances was detained on a charge of murder!

The Court Proceedings

On October 13, 2013, Frances Hall was arraigned in Bexar County Court, state of Texas, on charges of murder and aggravated assault with a deadly weapon. Frances entered a plea of "*not guilty*" and requested a jury trial. Bond was set at $225,000, and Frances was able to post bond and be released from custody with the provision that she wear an "ankle bracelet" while she was out on bail. Frances selected Adam Cortez to represent her on the assault and first-degree murder charges.

Texas v. Hall (The Jury Trial)

The jury trial for Frances Hall, after a delay of almost three years, was finally set for trial on August 30, 2016. The state of Texas, charged with the burden of proof in the case, presented the evidence. The state was represented by Stephanie Paulisen and Scott Simpson. The state presented testimony from several members of law enforcement including Texas Rangers and deputies with the Bexar County Sheriff's Office. Evidence presented by law enforcement including pictures and videos from the scene of the accident showing the Harley-Davidson motorcycle that was smashed and lying on the side of the road of Texas State Highway 1604. An employee of the Texas coroner's office presented testimony about the autopsy of Bill Hall, concluding that the death of Bill Hall was caused by blunt-force trauma to his head, neck, and back. The injuries, the coroner's office concluded, were consistent with trauma caused by being involved in a high-speed motor vehicle accident. The state also called an "expert witness," Timothy Lovett, who was considered an expert in "accident reconstruction" cases. Mr. Lovett testified that the physical evidence from the involved vehicles indicated that Frances Hall's Cadillac Escalade rammed the Range Rover being driven by Bonnie Contreras at least three or four times, causing extensive damage to the back of the Range Rover and the front of the Cadillac Escalade. Lovett also noted that there damage to the back of the Escalade, indicating that Bill's motorcycle had struck the back and side of the Escalade as it was chasing the Range Rover down the highway. The star witness for the state was Bonnie Contreras. Bonnie testified that the Cadillac Escalade, being driven by Frances Hall, chased her down State Highway 1604 for more than fifteen miles, repeatedly ramming the back of her car. Bonnie stated that during the chase, Frances collided with Bill's motorcycle, causing him to crash. Bonnie identified Frances as the woman who killed Bill Hall on October 10, 2013! The state rested its case.

The Defense of Francis Hall

The defense evidence focused on the conduct of Bonnie Contreras leading up to the date of the accident that killed Bill Hall. Bonnie was forced to admit that she had a three-year love affair with Bill that started in 2010. Bonnie had to admit that Bill bought her several expenses gifts including a sports car and a large diamond ring. Bonnie also admitted that Bill paid over $10,000 for plastic surgery to enhance her figure and appeal as an "exotic dancer." After three years, Bonnie grew tired of the "girlfriend arrangement"! She wanted Bill to get a divorce and marry her. Bill kept dragging his feet and putting her off. Bonnie admitted that she got Frances's phone number from Bill's cellphone and started sending Frances text messages, telling Frances that Bill was unhappy and he wanted to get a divorce. Bonnie even admitted that she sent "X-rated" pictures of herself with Bill, naked in bed and having sexual relations! The defense also presented evidence from its own "accident reconstruction" expert, Charles Ruble. Mr. Ruble testified that Bill was traveling along Texas State Highway 1604, following the vehicles being driven by Bonnie Contreras and Frances Hall. That at some point in the chase, Bill lost control of his motorcycle, veering off the road. Bill tried to correct his path back onto the roadway when he lost control of his vehicle and crashed into the back of Frances Hall's Cadillac Escalade, hitting the back window of the Cadillac. Ruble used photos from the accident scene of the Cadillac to support his conclusion: that Frances Hall was not at fault in the accident. The final witness for the defense was Hank Hall, a cousin of Bill Hall. Hank testified that Bill and he were very close friends growing up, that Bill confided in Hank that he was having an "extramarital affair" with Bonnie, and that he was trying to get rid of her! She was driving Bill crazy! Hank stated that, in his opinion, Frances did not kill Bill—that Bonnie was the one responsible for it!

The Jury Verdict

After a trial that spanned ten days, both parties rested in the case of *Texas v. Frances Hall*. After a closed door hearing between the judge and the attorneys representing the state and the defense, the judge reconvened the trial and gave the jury their final instructions relative to the evidence and the witnesses. The jury retired and began their deliberations. The jury deliberations continued all through the day and late into the evening. At about 9:00 p.m., the jury advised the bailiff that they had a verdict. The judge reconvened the court and summoned the jury to return to the courtroom. The jury verdict was handed to the judge who read the verdict: "In the district court of Bexar County, state of Texas, the *State of Texas v. Frances Hall*: we, the jury, duly empaneled to hear the evidence in the above-entitled cause do hereby find the defendant, Frances Hall, to be *'guilty'* of the crime of murder and assault with a deadly weapon!" The courtroom was silent! The people were stunned by the verdict. Frances Hall collapsed in her chair. The judge advised the jury that the verdict concluded the first phase of the case. The judge directed the jury to return to the courtroom a few days later to determine punishment. Frances Hall faced a possible punishment from a minimum of two years up to life in prison. Four days later, the jury returned to the courtroom to hear evidence about punishment Frances Hail should receive. The state presented its evidence, demanding that Frances Hall be given a minimum of twenty-five years in prison. The defense countered with its evidence from character witnesses, asking for leniency. The jury found that Frances acted with "sudden passion," giving Frances the minimum sentence of two years in prison. The people in the courtroom were shocked! Bonnie Contreras ran out of the courtroom in total disbelief! Frances's family was relieved. Frances gasped for air, in total shock!

The Sentence of the Court

On September 12, 2016, Frances Hall was sentenced to serve two years with the Texas Department of Corrections. Frances was sent to the Texas prison for women to complete her sentence of two years in prison. Finally, in September 2018, Frances was released from the Texas Department of Corrections to go home to be with her family. Almost three years of "legal hell" had been dumped on Frances Hall, following the death of her beloved husband. Tragically, the Bill Hall Trucking Company collapsed and filed for Chapter 7 bankruptcy, during the years that Frances was entangled in the murder charges filed against her. The assets of the company were liquidated, and more than a hundred people lost their jobs as a result of the Hall family tragedy. Frances and her daughter, Nikki, have remained together during the entire ordeal. However, her son, Jason, has become estranged from the rest of the family. Bonnie Contreras, Bill Hall's mistress, has publicly lambasted the Hall family, claiming that justice was not properly served by allowing a killer like Frances to run around loose after only two years in prison. Bonnie Contreras later filed a "wrongful death" lawsuit against Frances Hall, claiming that Frances owed her more than $1,000,000 in damages as a result of the auto accident that occurred on October 10, 2013. The case was later dismissed by the Texas courts.

Analysis of the Frances Hall Case

The automobile accident on October 10, 2013, is an American tragedy. Texas law enforcement authorities arrested Frances Hall at the scene of the accident and pushed for the prosecutors for the state to file "murder charges" against her immediately. Consider these factors that could be construed to be a "miscarriage of justice" in the Frances Hall case:

1. The defendant was charged with the crime of murder in the district court of Bexar County, Oklahoma. Was this proper charge? No! There was no evidence of premeditation on the part of Frances Hall. The most viable charge in this case would have been a charge of manslaughter. Considering the circumstances, the proper charge should have been second-degree manslaughter, a less serious charge that carries a maximum punishment of no more than five years' imprisonment in most states. The prosecution overcharged Frances Hall with the intent of putting her away for the rest of her life in the Texas State Department of Corrections.

2. The jury in the Frances Halt case, in the punishment phase of the trial, concluded that Frances acted with "sudden passion" after finding her husband driving down Texas State Highway 1604, following his "mistress," Bonnie Contreras, to an unknown location. What would any wife do under similar circumstances? Chase her husband down the highway to see where they were going? The state should have considered the "extenuating circumstances" existing in the case prior to the filing of any criminal charges. The state failed to do this! The jury made the ultimate decision that spared Frances from spending the rest of her life in a Texas prison.

3. The credibility of the witnesses in the case. Who was the principal witness for the state in its case against Frances Hall? Bonnie Contreras! The

same woman who had carried on an "immoral relationship" with Frances's husband for more than three years. Bonnie Contreras was the same woman who sent" X-rated texts" to Frances Hall, intending to inflict "emotional distress" on Frances Hall until she had a nervous breakdown! That is exactly what happened on October 10, 2013!

Truly, the Hall case is a miscarriage of justice that should have never occurred in America!

THE SOUTH CAROLINA KILLER
South Carolina v. Debra Sheridan (2017)

Debra Sheridan was born in Anderson County, South Carolina, in 1965. Being a lady from the south, Debra loved the outdoors and life in the country. Debra was very fond of animals, dogs and cats and horses. After completing her education, Debra worked for on a ranch and saved her money. Eventually, Debra was able to purchase an acreage of her own. Within five years, Debra was able to set up an animal rescue place which she named the Golden S Ranch. With the help of charitable donations from churches and animal rescue organizations, Debra was able to construct three buildings on the property to house starving and abandoned animals. Within five years, Debra was the head of one of the largest animal rescue organizations in South Carolina. The Golden S Ranch would typically house more than a hundred animals during a normal month. The work was overwhelming! Debra was frequently exhausted at the end of a day's work. Debra, after much thought, concluded that she needed to hire some help in order to properly run the ranch. Debra placed an ad in the local papers, offering a position of employment for a caretaker for her animals. One day, a man named Jerry Sanders showed up, telling Debra that he had seen the ad in the paper. Debra told Jerry that the pay was minimal but that he would have room and board, staying in one of the barns which were used to house the animals. Being unemployed, Jerry took the job. Jerry moved in and started taking care of the animals, setting out hay and food for them.

The operations at the Golden S Ranch ran very smoothly for a few months. When Debra was attending fund-raising events all over the state of South Carolina, Jerry would remain on the ranch and take care of the animals. Debra was invited to attend a national meeting of an "animal rights" advocacy group in California. Debra accepted the invitation, feeling that Jerry would take good care of the ranch while she was gone for several days. Debra gave Jerry a list of supplies to get for the ranch while she was gone, along with $500 to take care of the expenses of operating the ranch while she was gone. Debra traveled to the Golden State, having full confidence that the ranch was in good hands while she was gone. Debra enjoyed a successful trip, filled with information and great ideas for future fund-raising for her ranch operations. Debra returned home late one evening after the weeklong trip to California and headed to bed, exhausted from the six-hour plane ride from California. Arising early the next morning, Debra went out to the barns to check on her animals and Jerry. Entering the barn, Debra could tell that something was wrong! The animals were restless and appeared to have not been fed for several days. Debra checked Jerry's room. No one was there. The room was a mess with trash everywhere including empty beer and liquor bottles all over the place. The bed looked like it had not been slept in for several days. After taking care of the animals, Debra looked everywhere on the ranch for Jerry. He was nowhere to be found! Looking in the garage, Debra noticed that her pickup was also missing. Returning to the house, Debra picked up the phone to call the sheriff's office. Suddenly, Jerry drove up in her truck and walked into the house. After Jerry offered several flimsy excuses about what where he had been, Debra fired Jerry and told him to leave her property. Jerry gathered his belongings and headed out, telling Debra that she would be very sorry!

The Date of the Murder (January 21, 2017)

Early the next morning, Debra got up early, anticipating a "busy day," getting things back in order around the ranch. Restocking the grain bins and the water tanks with fresh water took most of the morning. Debra spent the afternoon cleaning up the mess that Jerry had left in the living quarters and in the barns. Debra had just returned to the house when she got a call from a lady friend, inviting her out to dinner. Debra gladly accepted. She needed a "hot meal" after a long day at work. After cleaning up with a nice warm bath, Debra put on a fresh set of clothes and headed into town. Debra left the ranch around 5:00 p.m. Debra enjoyed a delightful evening out, dining on steak and lobster. Debra decided to head home at 7:30 p.m., tired from her long day at the ranch. Debra drove up to her house and exited her car. As she was getting out of her car, Debra thought that she heard a noise coming the barn. Debra glanced down at the barn and heard a "loud crash" like someone was in the barn. Debra walked into her house and retrieved a gun from a drawer in her kitchen. Debra came out of the house and headed down toward the barn. Hearing another noise coming from the barn, Debra fired a "warning shot" up into the air. Debra noticed that one of the windows in the front area of the barn was open. Debra fired a second shot up into the air above the barn. At that point, a man jumped out from behind a nearby bush and started running toward her. Debra fired a third shot at the man, hitting him in the chest and killing him!

Debra hesitated for a moment, not sure what she should do. Debra slowly walked up to the man lying on ground. Looking down at the body, Debra noticed that the man was dressed in dark clothing with a "face covering" over his head. Debra bent down and removed the mask. She stepped back in a "state of disbelief." The man lying on the ground was Jerry Sanders! Reflecting back for a moment, Debra remembered his last words before he left: "You will be very sorry!" Gathering her senses, Debra turned and ran back to the house.

Debra picked up the phone and dialed 911. A deputy with the Anderson County Sheriff's Office was dispatched to the scene of the shooting. Debra called two of her friends to come out to the ranch as she awaited the arrival of the sheriff's office.

Upon arrival, the deputy determined that the shooting victim was deceased and summoned the coroner's office to come to the scene. Within a few minutes, Anderson County Sheriff Chad McBride arrived at the scene and supervised the investigation. Debra was questioned about the events leading up to the shooting. Debra related that she had been out to dinner with friends. That upon her return to the house, she heard noises coming from the barn.

Retrieving her gun, Debra went out to investigate. Debra related that a man dressed in dark clothing and wearing a mask over his face to conceal his identity jumped out from behind a bush near the barn and ran toward her. Debra stated that she raised her gun and fired one shot, striking the man in the chest. The man fell to the ground immediately.

Debra stated that she did not realize who the man was until she walked over and took off his face mask. Debra identified the man as Jerry Sanders, a former ranch employee that she had recently fired due to "employee misconduct": drinking on the job.

Sheriff McBride completed his investigation at the scene of the crime, advising Debra that he wanted her to come to the sheriff's office the next morning at 10:00 a.m. Debra spent the night with one of her friends and went to the sheriff's office the next morning. Debra was questioned for more than two hours by the sheriff with regard to the events on the night of the shooting and the prior contacts that she had had with the deceased, Jerry Sanders. At the conclusion of the extensive interrogation, Debra signed a sworn statement and was allowed to leave. The sheriff advised Debra that the sheriff's office would conduct a thorough investigation and confer with the prosecutor's office relative to the possible charges that could be filed in connection with the homicide. The law enforcement investigation continued on for more than six months. Debra felt mounting anxiety that she was going to be charged with murder. Finally, on August 2, 2017, the sheriff of Anderson County held a press conference. Present at the news conference was a representative of the Solicitor General's Office of the state of South Carolina. Sheriff McBride stated that "*no charges*" would be filed against Debra Sheridan related to the homicide of Jeffrey Sanders. The sheriff related that Debra was acting "in self-defense" when she shot and killed Sanders on January 21, 2017. Sheriff McBride stated that the shooting occurred on Debra's property and that under the law of South Carolina, Debra had the right to "stand her ground" and use "deadly force" against anyone who threatened her personal safety. The sheriff concluded that it was a case of "justifiable homicide." Finally, Debra Sheridan could relax and enjoy her life after six months of a "living hell"!

Analysis of the Debra Sheridan Case

The Sheridan case is not unusual in America today. Every day, property owners are faced with the dilemma of what to do when a person comes on their property and proceeds to commit a crime. In the Sheridan case, Debra was confronted by an angry ex-employee whom she fired for misconduct, drinking on the job. The former employee, Jerry Sanders, threatened her when she fired him the day before. In retaliation, Jerry Sanders came back on her ranch the following day and was in the process of stealing and vandalizing her property when she returned home after dinner with her friends. Debra was required, under the circumstances, to retrieve her gun and shoot the man in her front yard as he was charging toward her. To protect her own personal safety, Debra was forced to shoot and kill Jerry Sanders in front of her house. The case was clearly one of "justifiable homicide." The puzzling aspect of the Sheridan case is, Why did it take more than six months for the state to decide that no charges should be filed in the case? Tragically, a lot of cases like the Sheridan case happen on a regular basis in America today. The criminal justice moves very slowly when there a homicide where the property owner kills an intruder who came on their property with the intent to commit a serious crime.

KILLING A CHILD MOLESTER
Washington v. Yvonne Wanrow (1972)

Yvonne Wanrow was born on the Colville Indian Reservation outside of Inchelium, Washington, during the early 1940s. Yvonne attended the public schools in Colville, graduating from Colville High School in 1961. Immediately after graduating from high school, Yvonne got married to RJ, her high school sweetheart. Within the three years, Yvonne had two children, a son and a daughter. Her husband, RJ, left her for another woman. Yvonne got a divorce, gaining custody of her two small children. Being a member of the Colville tribe, she applied to the Bureau of Indian Affairs for a grant to further her education. The BIA approved her request for financial aid, and she moved to San Francisco, California, to study fashion design. Yvonne was forced to leave her children in the custody of her parents while she attended school. Yvonne successfully completed her studies in fashion design and went to work in San Francisco. A few months later, her daughter suddenly died of encephalitis at the age of three years old. Her ex-husband joined her for the funeral services to say goodbye to their little daughter. The couple reconciled and subsequently moved to Oregon.

After a few months, the couple separated again and went their separate ways. Yvonne decided to move back home to be near her parents. Yvonne settled in Spokane, Washington. For the first few months, Yvonne lived with her sister. Eventually, she found a job and moved into a rent house. Since Yvonne worked during the evening hours, she allowed her two children to be cared for by a neighbor named Shirley Hooper. The kids would stay with Mrs. Hooper during the evening hours, and Yvonne would pick them up after she got off work in the morning. While in the Hooper household, one of Yvonne's children complained to Hooper that a man named William Wesler had approached him in a neighborhood park and tried to lure him into a nearby house. Once inside the house, Wesler closed the door and tried to assault the young child. Somehow, the boy was able to escape and run to safety!

The Date of the Murder (August 12, 1972)

Yvonne arrived home from work and went next door to pick up her kids. Mrs. Hooper advised Yvonne about the police being called out after the assault by Wesler. A complaint to the local police about the assault resulted in an officer coming out to the scene and taking a "citizen's complaint" about Wesler. The police went over the neighbor's to confront Wesler about the alleged assault. Wesler denied the allegations made by Yvonne's son. The police left the area without arresting Wesler, concluding that there was insufficient evidence to warrant the arrest of an otherwise law-abiding citizen! Yvonne took her kids home to rest for a few hours. She invited Hooper to come over and spend the night at her house. Yvonne had a gun, and she knew how to use it! Hooper accepted the invitation and came over to Yvonne's the following evening, arriving before dark.

With the two families at Yvonne's house, the ladies took turns watching the front door. At approximately 5:00 a.m., Yvonne was awakened by a noise near the front of the house. Yvonne retrieved her pistol from a nearby nightstand and hid in a closet near the living room of the house. The knob on the front door turned and suddenly a dark figure in dark-colored clothing entered the door.

Hooper yelled, "Get out of here!" Ignoring the order, Wesler entered the house. All the kids were awakened by the noise. Instead of leaving, Wesler came into the house and approached the crying children. Yvonne slowly opened the closet door and raised her pistol, pointing it at Wesler as he approached the children lying on the floor. Yvonne pulled the trigger of the gun, *bam*!

Wesler slumped to the floor and passed out. With a fatal gunshot wound to his chest, Wesley passed away within a few minutes.

Hooper rushed to the phone and dialed 911. When the operator came on the line, "Nine, one, one, what is your emergency?" Hooper stated, "A man has just been shot over here! I think that he is dead. Send the police immediately!"

The Police Investigation

A police officer arrived at Yvonne's house within about ten minutes. Examining the dead body lying on the living room floor, the officer asked all the people inside the house to step outside to "preserve the crime scene." Within a few minutes, the shift commander arrived and had the occupants placed in two different police vehicles to obtain statements from the individual parties. Yvonne admitted to the officers that she heard a noise outside her house and she grabbed her gun, hiding in a nearby closet. Yvonne stated that when the door opened, a man in dark clothing entered the house. Mrs. Hooper yelled at the man, "Get out of here!" The man ignored the warning and approached the children laying on the floor. The man reached down and started to grab Yvonne's son. Yvonne stated that she came out of the closet, pointed her gun at the man, and fired one shot. *Bam!* The man was struck by the bullet and fell to the floor in the living room. Mrs. Hooper then called 911 to the police department. The police arrested Yvonne and took her to the police station. Yvonne was booked into jail and subsequently charged with the crime of murder. The local police department conducted a background on Yvonne. The records check revealed that Yvonne had no prior criminal record and that she had never been charged with a crime in the American legal system. Doing the same type of records check on the deceased, the police uncovered some interesting information. First, William Wesler had been previously been convicted on "child molestation" charges. Second, the deceased had been confined to the Eastern State Hospital of Washington for several months after a court had had conducted a "competency hearing" and determined that he had a significant mental illness!

The Court Proceedings

Yvonne was formally charged with the crime of first-degree murder in August 1972. During the formal arraignment, Yvonne entered a plea of "not guilty" and requested a trial by jury. Since Yvonne qualified for a court-appointed counsel, the trial judge appointed her an attorney from the public defender's office. Several weeks later, a show-cause hearing was conducted in the circuit court in Spokane, Washington. At the conclusion of the hearing, Yvonne was ordered to stand trial on an amended charge of second-degree murder. The public defender's representative, after reviewing all the evidence that the state had presented at the show-cause hearing, advised Yvonne to enter a plea of "guilty" to the charge of second-degree murder. Yvonne complained about the lawyer appointed to represent her. The trial court subsequently appointed a new attorney, not associated with the local public defender office, to represent her in the murder case. After reviewing all the evidence, the new attorney advised Yvonne to withdraw her "guilty" plea and demand a trial by jury. At the jury trial in May 1973, the jury selection process resulted in a jury panel of twelve men, all White, to hear the evidence and render a verdict in the case. During the early 1970s, the militant actions of the American Indian Movement were extensively covered by the print and electronic media in the state of Washington. The media coverage was very "negative" toward the Native America Tribes located inside the state of Washington. Yvonne's trial was set during this turbulent era. The defense presented evidence that Yvonne had a right of self-defense when the intruder, William Wesler, entered her house during the early morning hours of August 12, 1972. The all-male jury panel ignored this evidence and found Yvonne guilty of second-degree murder, recommending a sentence of twenty years in prison!

The Appeals of Yvonne Wanrow

The defense counsel for Yvonne filed an appeal of her conviction to the Washington Criminal Court of Appeals. The defense's appeal was based on several counts of judicial error by the trial judge and jury. In August 1975, the appellate court reversed Yvonne's conviction and ordered a new trial on several grounds of error by the trial judge. The errors of the trial judge included the following:

1. The trial judge failed to sequester the jury during the trial proceedings. Members of the jury were allowed to go home at night and read the newspapers and watch local television news. The appellate court declared that this failure to sequester the jury violated the fundamental rights of Yvonne under the Sixth Amendment: "to a fair trial by a fair and impartial jury"!

2. The coerced confession that Yvonne gave the police on the morning of the murder had violated her rights under her Fifth Amendment of the US Constitution.

3. The trial judge had given improper and inadequate instructions to the jury with regard to the defendant's right of self-defense under the facts and circumstances of the case.

The state prosecutors filed an appeal to the Washington Supreme Court. In 1977, the Supreme Court denied the state's appeal, concluding that Yvonne was, indeed, entitled to a new trial before a different trial judge based on the errors made by the trial court in the original jury trial. While awaiting a new trial, Yvonne entered a plea of "guilty" to a reduced charge of manslaughter. Yvonne was sentenced to five years' imprisonment, with the time to be suspended after the completion of community service. Yvonne was finally free at last, after five years of living though a legal nightmare!

Analysis of the Yvonne Wanrow Case

The criminal prosecution of Yvonne Wanrow in connection with the shooting death of William Wesler is an American tragedy. The case should have never been filed! The incident related to the death of Wesler was clearly a case of "justifiable homicide." Every American citizen has the right to use "deadly force" when an unknown intruder enters their home and poses a threat the safety of the homeowner or their immediate family. In this case, a convicted felon, William Wesler, was entering Yvonne's home at five o'clock in the morning intending to kidnap or do bodily harm to one of Yvonne's children. The criminal prosecution of Yvonne was a prime example of "prosecutorial misconduct" and "judicial misconduct" that should never occur in the American legal system. As noted in the opinion of the Washington Court of Criminal Appeals, Yvonne's constitutional rights were violated in several respects, to wit,

1.   The confession given by Yvonne to the local police was coerced, so it was in violation of her rights under the Fifth Amendment and the doctrine outlined by the United States Supreme Court in the case of *Miranda v. Arizona (1966)*.

2.   The trial judge did not order the sequestration of the jury that was hearing the case, thereby violating Yvonne's rights under the Sixth Amendment, depriving Yvonne of her right to have a trial by a fair and impartial jury. The mistake of the trial court totally contradicted the rules established by the United States Supreme Court in the case of *Sheppard v. Maxwell (1966)*.

3.   Yvonne did not receive a fair trial, since the jury was composed of White men, which is a case of prosecutor misconduct because he challenged and removed any woman from the jury panel. This is in violation of the doctrine outlined by the United States Supreme Court in the case of *Furman v. Georgia (1972)*.

Clearly, Yvonne's case is a "miscarriage of justice" that should never have occurred in America!

MURDER IN ALABAMA
Alabama v. Jacqueline Dixon (2018)

The Facts of the Case

At approximately 8:30 a.m. on July 31, 2018, a call was placed to 911 for the Selma, Alabama, police department. A woman's voice on the line stated, "I just shot a man in my front yard! I think he is dead!" The 911 operator inquired, "Are you okay?" "I am okay," the woman replied. "I am shocked at having to shot an intruder!" The 911 operator assured the woman that everything would be okay. "I am dispatching an officer to your location. He should be there in fifteen minutes." A patrol officer with the Selma, Alabama, arrived at the scene of the shooting, a house located at 2113 Church Street in Selma. Upon arriving, the officer found a Black male, forty-four-year-old Carl Dixon, lying in the grass in the front yard of the house. Selma Police Chief Spenser Collier arrived shortly afterward. Chief Collier went up to the front porch of the residence where Jacqueline Dixon was standing. Chief Collier interviewed Jacqueline, asking her about what happened. Jacqueline advised Chief Collier that Carl Dixon showed up at her house that morning and started threatening her, telling her that he was going to kill her. During the argument, Jacqueline pulled a small-caliber handgun out of her purse and told Dixon to leave her property. Dixon refused to leave, approaching her with his fists clinched, getting ready to hit her. Jacqueline fired her gun and shot Carl, *bam! bam!*

Chief Collier asked about the weapon she had used. Jacqueline pulled a small pistol out of her purse which Chief Collier recognized to be a .22-caliber pistol. Chief Collier directed that the gun be placed in an "evidence bag" to be sent to the state authorities for a forensic examination. Chief Collier directed his officers to escort Jacqueline to the Selma police station for further questioning while he secured the crime scene and awaited the coroner's office to arrive and take charge of the remains of the victim, Carl Dixon. The police department completed their investigation and forwarded their report to the Dallas County District Attorney's Office. The Alabama Bureau of Investigation conducted its examination of the gun taken from Jacqueline Dixon. Their report concluded that Jacqueline Dixon's handgun was, in fact, the murder weapon. The report from the coroner's office confirmed that Carl Dixon's death was caused by blunt-force trauma, two gunshots to the chest by a small-caliber weapon.

Under the law of Alabama, the prosecutor cannot automatically file a felony charge in state court against a person suspected of a crime. The prosecutor's office is required to petition the presiding district judge to convene a grand jury to listen to the evidence collected by law enforcement and determine whether a crime has been committed.

The grand jury is composed of twelve citizens of the county who listen to the evidence and decide whether a criminal charge should be filed against the party responsible for the felony crime. If the grand jury concludes that there is sufficient evidence, the grand jury panel can return an "indictment" formally charging the person with the crime. The Dallas County Court ordered a grand jury hearing in regard to the murder of Carl Dixon.

The Grand Jury Investigation

On October 12, 2018, a grand jury was convened in Dallas County, Alabama, to hear evidence relative to the murder of Carl Dixon. Police officers with the Selma Police Department testified as to the events on July 31, 2018: the 911 call; the crime scene when the officers arrived; and the confiscation of the murder weapon, a .22-caliber pistol. Police Chief Collier testified about the statement Jacqueline gave at the scene of the crime. Chief Collier testified that Jacqueline admitted that she had shot the victim when he refused to leave her property.

Taking the stand in her own defense, Jacqueline testified that she had been married to the victim, Carl Dixon. After ten years of marriage, they separated and Carl moved out of the house. Jacqueline further testified that Carl would often return to the house uninvited and express his anger with regard to the ongoing domestic dispute between the parties. Jacqueline was forced to go to court in 2016 and get a "restraining order" against Carl, prohibiting him from coming around Jacqueline and their two kids. On several occasions, Carl would show up at the house and beg to be allowed to return to the house and live there with his kids. Jacqueline refused and told him to leave. On the morning of July 31, Carl showed up at the house shortly after 8:00 a.m. Carl appeared to be intoxicated and told her that he was going to beat "the hell" out of her if she did not let him back in the house. Jacqueline ordered Carl to leave. He refused! He came charging toward her with his fists clinched, telling her that he was going to kill her. Jacqueline indicated, that at that point, she pulled out her small handgun and shot Carl twice as he ran toward her with clinched fists.

At the conclusion of the defense presentation of evidence to the grand jury, her defense counsel argued that the Stand Your Ground Law applied in the case, that the grand jury should decline to recommend criminal charges be pursued against Jacqueline Dixon.

The state of Alabama legislature passed the Stand Your Ground Law in 2006, which states that homeowners are not required "to retreat" from their home if they are faced with an "imminent danger" to the personal safety of themselves or their children. Defense Attorney Richard Rice argued that the victim, Carl Dixon, showed up at her house on the morning of July 31, 2018, and started threatening her with physical violence; that Carl Dixon was, at the time, under a "restraining order" which prohibited him from having any contact with Jacqueline or the children; and that under those circumstances, Jacqueline was justified in using "deadly force" to protect herself and her children. The presiding judge gave specific instructions to the grand jury for their guidance in weighing the evidence presented to them both by the state and the defense counsel. After several hours of deliberations behind closed doors, the grand jury returned to open court and issued the following statement: "We, the grand jury, impaneled to hear evidence in the case of *Alabama v. Jacqueline Dixon*, find that there is NO BASIS under the evidence presented to order an indictment against Jacqueline Dixon with regard to the death of Carl Dixon that occurred on July 31, 2018."

The presiding judge accepted the findings of the grand jury and ordered that Jacqueline Dixon be released from custody and her bond exonerated. Jacqueline Dixon was allowed to resume a normal life. Jacqueline is currently working, serving as a real estate broker in the state of Alabama.

Analysis of the Jacqueline Dixon Case

One of fundamentals principles defined in the Fifth Amendment of the United States Constitution is the right of citizens to be protected from prosecutor misconduct and abuse in the criminal justice system. The Fifth Amendment requires that the charges in a criminal case must be by "indictment" issued by a grand jury panel of citizens in the community where the accused person lives. The grand jury panel is charged with the responsibility of listening to the evidence presented by the government authorities to determine whether a person should be charged with a crime. In the Alabama case involving Jacqueline Dixon, the state of Alabama was required to show all the evidence that law enforcement had collected in reference to the murder of Carl Dixon. Both the state and the defense were allowed to present evidence to the jury. The jury panel decided, based on the facts and circumstances surrounding the death of Carl Dixon, that Jacqueline was justified in using "deadly force" to shoot and kill Carl Dixon in the front yard of her residence when he came onto her property and threatened her on the morning of July 31, 2018. The Alabama Stand Your Ground Law allowed Jacqueline to pull her gun out and shoot Carl before he could reach her front door and injure her with his clinched fists. The jury panel made the right decision! Jacqueline Dixon deserved to be exonerated and allowed to get on with her life, taking care of her two children.

THE PINE STREET SHOOTOUT!
Oklahoma v. Erin Dukes (1997)

Erin Colleen Lewis was born in Tulsa, Oklahoma, in 1973. After graduating from high school, Erin decided to take a job out of state. Erin moved to the state of Florida, obtaining a job in the field of criminal justice. Erin met a man at work named Lee Dukes. Lee was considerably older than Erin and appeared to be a very nice gentleman with great manners and a warm smile. The couple started dating and eventually got married. Within a year, the couple was blessed with the birth of a young boy. A year later, Erin gave birth to a second boy. With two small boys to raise, Erin's days were consumed with taking care of the boys. Lee grew angry and resentful. Upon getting home from work, Lee would start drinking and often down a six-pack of beer during the evening. Once Lee was drunk, he would become abusive toward Erin and the boys. On weekends, Lee's behavior would get worse.

Lee would get upset with Erin and grab her up, shaking her and threatening to slap the kids around. After a few weeks of escalating abuse, Erin decided to take the boys and return back to Oklahoma to be near her parents. Erin packed up her belongings along with the kid's stuff and headed back to Tulsa while Lee was at work one day. Erin, with the help of her parents, found a nice house to live in located on East Pine Street in Tulsa, Oklahoma. Her new home was located a short distance from her parents' house. Erin's mom could take care of the boys while she worked. Life seemed to be great again. Then Lee showed up out of the blue one day!

Lee apologized for his abusive behavior and asked for forgiveness. Lee told Erin that he had given up drinking and that he was a changed man. Erin, being a compassionate young woman, relented and allowed Lee to move in with her and the kids in the house on Pine Street. Within a few days, Lee got a job at a large maintenance facility. Erin had a good-paying job as a corrections officer at the Avalon Corrections Center in Tulsa. Life appeared to be getting better for Erin and the kids. However, appearances can be deceiving!

Erin realized in a few months that Lee had not given up his drinking habits.

Lee would stop at a neighborhood bar and have several beers before heading home for the evening. He would arrive home, often bringing in a twelve-pack of beer with him.

Lee would drink twelve beers during the evening, becoming totally drunk. When Lee got drunk, he would turn angry and abusive, often striking tee and threatening the kids.

On September 12, 1997, Erin called the police on Lee, complaining that he was drunk and that he was assaulting her. When the Tulsa police responded to the call, they took an "offense report," noting that Erin had bruises on her arms and body. The officer inquired as to whether she wanted to file a complaint and have Lee arrested, thereby removing him from the house. Lee begged her not to! Erin relented and told the officers that "it is okay." The officer left the house without making an arrest. Lee apologized and went off to bed. Erin took the kids and went to stay with her parents for the evening. Things appeared to be returning to normal for a few weeks. That all changed within one month! Lee returned to old habits!

The Date of the Murder (October 15, 1997)

Lee's old habits: drinking ten to twelve cans of beer in the evening. Once Lee was drunk, the abusive behavior would return. Lee grabbed Erin and started hitting her in the chest with his fists. Erin was knocked back on the sofa. Taking a break, Lee grabbed another beer out of the refrigerator and gulped it down. During this moment of distraction, Erin reached for her purse. Standing up, Erin told Lee that it was "over! Get out of my house, now!" she yelled. Lee started toward her with his fist clutched, ready to hit her again. Reaching into her purse, Erin pulled out her .32-caliber pistol and fired it at Lee. *Bam! Bam! Bam! Bam!* Four buffets struck Lee in the chest, neck, and head! Lee slumped to the floor and was immediately unconscious. Erin immediately ran out the front door of the house and threw her service revolver down on the grass. Erin looked around for help. Seeing that one of her neighbors was home, Erin ran next door and called the Tulsa Police Department. Two officers from the police department arrived at the residence within fifteen minutes. Erin had sensed that there would be trouble that evening. She had taken her two young boys to her mother's house earlier in the day. The police officers secured the crime scene and determined that Lee was dead.

Erin was asked about what happened. Erin readily admitted that she had shot Lee after he had struck her several times earlier in the evening. After finding the gun lying in the yard, the police officer arrested Erin and transported her to the police station.

The Murder Trial of Erin Dukes

Erin was arrested on the evening of October 15, 1997, and transported to the Tulsa Police Department. Detective Kenneth McCoy took Erin into an interrogation room and questioned her about the events that led up to the shooting of her husband, Lee Dukes. Erin advised the detective that she was "the victim" of physical abuse by her husband and that Lee was drunk and started beating her, striking her several times in the chest and stomach. Erin told the officer that during the assault, she pulled out her gun, a .32-caliber pistol and shot Lee as he started to hit her again. Erin advised the detective that she was an armed CLEET-certified prison guard at the Avalon Correctional Center in Tulsa. Erin concluded her confession, telling Detective McCoy that she was "in fear of her life" when she pulled her gun out and shot Lee. The statement and confession was videotaped at the police department. Erin was formally arrested and booked into the Tulsa County Jail, the charge: murder in the first degree. During her arraignment two days later, Erin entered a plea of "not guilty" and requested a trial by jury. Prominent criminal defense attorney Mark Lyons was selected to represent Erin during the case.

A preliminary hearing was conducted several weeks later. The presiding judge ordered the district attorney to file an amended complaint and information, charging Erin with the lesser charge of first-degree manslaughter. Erin was allowed to post bond in the amount of $25,000 and was released from the Tulsa County Jail. Erin Dukes was forced to wait two years before the case finally was brought up fora jury trial.

Finally, on a cool winter day in February 2000, the case of Erin Dukes came on for a jury trial in the district court of Tulsa County, Oklahoma. The judge assigned to the case was District Judge Jesse Harris. A jury panel of twelve citizens of Tulsa County was selected to serve on the jury. The prosecutor presented the testimony of several members of the Tulsa Police Department related to the events that transpired on the evening of October 15, 1997, at the Dukes home. Detective McCoy of the Tulsa Police Department presented the videotaped confession of Erin taken at the interrogation room of the Tulsa Police Department. The medical examiner presented testimony that the victim sustained four gunshot wounds to the head, neck, and chest, and that Lee Dukes died almost immediately. The state rested its case at that point in the trial.

The defense of Erin focused on the long and troubled history of Lee Dukes. Attorney Mark Lyons presented evidence that Lee had "brutalized people" for more than twenty years. Evidence showed that Lee Dukes had beaten up his ex-wife and an ex-girlfriend when he lived in Florida, several years before he had met and married Erin. The defense then presented testimony by an "expert witness," Ashley Fuller, director of Tulsa office of the Domestic Violence Intervention Center. Mrs. Fuller testified she had conducted an extensive forensics examination of the Erin Dukes case and that in her expert opinion, Erin Dukes was the classic example of a woman being the victim of an abusive spouse. Mrs. Fuller concluded that Erin suffered from the battered women's syndrome.

In that regard, Erin felt that the only way out of the marriage was to use "deadly force"! That happened on the evening of October15, 1997, when she shot and killed Lee!

The Jury Verdict

At the conclusion of the defense evidence, Judge Harris recessed the trial to conduct an "in-camera" hearing in his chambers with regard to the instructions to be given to the jury. A record was made with the court reporter being present to take down the remarks of the judge and the counsel for both the state and the defense. Upon reconvening the court, Judge Harris gave instructions to the jury relating to the "burden of proof" being on the state to prove the case beyond a "reasonable doubt" and that the defendant was "presumed innocent" of the charges. Judge Harris gave additional instructions that the jury would have to review the evidence and consider one of three options: (1) Was the defendant guilty of first-degree manslaughter? (2) Was the defendant guilty of the crime of second-degree manslaughter? Or (3) was the defendant was guilty of any crime? After final closing arguments from both the attorneys, the jury retired to begin their deliberations. Approximately three hours later, the jury notified the court bailiff that they had reached a verdict. Judge Harris reconvened the court, and the jury was seated. The foreman of the jury handed the verdict forms to the bailiff who delivered the forms to the judge.

After examining the verdict, Judge Harris stated, "Erin Hughes, please rise!" Getting to her feet, Erin turned and faced the jury. Judge Harris read the verdict as follows:

"We, the jury, duly sworn to serve as the jury in this case, find the Defendant, Erin Dukes, 'NOT GUILTY' of any and all charges filed in the case herein. Erin Dukes was released and allowed to take her boys and go home, finally a "free woman"!

Analysis of the Erin Dukes Case

The jury verdict in the Erin Dukes reflects the opinion of the jury with regard to a woman being assaulted in her own home. The victim, Lee Dukes, had a long and violent history of abusing women. Dukes had physically abused his first wife several years earlier in Florida. Dukes subsequently abused an ex-girlfriend who filed criminal charges against him, causing him to lose his job. The jury may have considered additional factors in reaching their verdict. These factors include the following:

1. Lee was an abusive alcoholic! The evidence showed that he typically drank ten to twelve cans of beer every day. When Lee became drunk, he would become violent, often striking Erin with his clutched fists.

2. The shooting happened in Erin's house. The state of Oklahoma is a "Castle Law" state. A person's home is their castle. Every person inside their own home has the right to "use deadly force" against any person who poses an "imminent threat" to their personal safety. Erin demanded that Lee leave her house. Lee refused, approaching her with a clutched fist, getting ready to assault and beat her again. The jury concluded that at that point, Erin had the right to draw her .32-caliber pistol out of her purse and shoot Lee in her living room. Under these circumstances, Erin was justified in using deadly force to protect herself from further serious bodily injury.

The jury verdict in the Erin Dukes case reflects the fact that the shooting of Lee Dukes on October 15, 1997, was a case of "justifiable homicide." The unfortunate fact is that Erin Dukes spent more than two years of uncertainty awaiting her day in court. Clearly, a miscarriage of justice for a young lady who deserved better from the court system.

THE DEATH OF A TERRORIST
Maine v. Amber Cummings (2009)

Amber Cummings was born in a small town in Northern California in 1978. Being a very attractive, slender, dark-haired young lady, Amber attracted a lot of attention while in high school. Amber was shocked to receive so much attention from the young men in her class since she considered herself "an introvert" and very shy. During her senior year, Amber was introduced to a young man by the name of James Cummings. James was a quiet young man who was very polite to young ladies in her school. Amber was impressed by his quiet demeanor and beautiful smile.

James and Amber started dating during their last year in high school and became engaged, agreeing to get married after they graduated from high school. While Amber came from a working-class family, James had an entirely different childhood. James's father was a wealthy businessman who had amassed a large fortune from his various investments in real estate and the stock market. When his father passed away while James was in school, James was named as the primary beneficiary of a large multimillion trust that his father had established prior to his death. James's income from the trust was in excess of $100,000 per month. Amber imagined that she would live like the queen of England: a life of traveling, shopping, household servants, and hot sports car. That was Amber's vision of her future with her dream man, James. While dreams do come true, many marriages end up being a living "nightmare"!

James and Amber got married in 1997 in Northern California. Because they both liked the idea of travel and sightseeing, James bought a large recreational vehicle and took Amber on a tour of many of the tourist attractions in North America. After seeing the country for a couple of years, the newlyweds decided to settle down in Texas for a few years. Amber was happy to settle down since she had learned that she was expecting her first child.

In 2001, Amber gave birth to a beautiful daughter who the couple named Clara. Amber's dream of living a "fairy-tale life" was coming true! Deciding that the weather was too warm during the summer months, the couple decided to move to a cooler climate, settling in Belfast, Maine. James purchased a large two-story house, and the couple settled into their new environment, living in New England. The climate was analogous to the pleasant climate that they had enjoyed in Northern California. Amber was allowed to redecorate the house and pick out the furniture for it.

A special child's room was created for Clara. Amber enjoyed her new home and the small-town atmosphere of Belfast. James enjoyed his own private space, furnishing his area of the house with historical artifacts and books related to his favorite era, the 1930s and the 1940s. James was especially interested in the history of Nazi Germany and the writings of Adolf Hitler. James bought a large collection of Nazi flags, guns, and other collectables. James was a follower of the "White supremacy" movement in America. James would spend several hours of the day on his computer, following the online messaging of leading figures of "White supremacy" movement in North America.

James became active in the National Socialist Party (the Communist Party for North America), making payments to the party organization and receiving weekly briefings on the activities of the party. James would travel to party meetings in the New England area. The National Socialist Party was very active in the American presidential election for the year 2008.

James was very concerned about the outcome of the election and attended several party meetings during election year 2008. While James was away attending one meeting, Amber went through his personal effects and found dozens of videos and magazine containing "child pornography"! Apparently, James had an addiction to "child pornography." Amber confronted James when he returned home.

James admitted he "loved it" and forced Amber to watch "child porn" late in the evening after their daughter, Clara, had gone to bed. James would force Amber to engage in "kinky sex" after watching the child pornography. When Barack Obama won the presidential election in November 2008, James became very upset. James was obsessed! He had to do something to prevent Obama from being sworn into office in January 2009. Amber observed James spent six to eight hours each day talking on his cell phone with various party members around the country.

What could be done to stop Barack Obama? Amber noticed that James was also ordering a great deal of stuff off the Internet and having it delivered to the house. James would always grab the packages when they arrived and take them to his area of the house and lock the room. James was examining the delivered items and placing them in a large walk-in closet next his bedroom. Amber wondered what all these items were and what he was going to do.

The Day of the Murder (December 9, 2008)

During the holiday season in the fall of 2008, while most families were enjoying the season, James became "paranoid," expressing his concern that someone was out to get him! As James's behavior became more bizarre each passing day, Amber became concerned that James was going to kill her and force Clara to be subjected to being exposed to child pornography. Amber contemplated "suicide" to end the nightmare that she was experiencing. Amber realized that if she did commit suicide, Clara would be forced to be James's sex slave. Suicide was not the answer! Amber thought about taking Clara and leaving during the night after James went to bed.

Amber concluded that was not the solution. She had tried to leave James on several prior occasions. Each time, James would hunt her down, drag her back to the house, and beat "the hell" out of her. There was only one viable solution, kill James!

On December 8, 2008, Amber got out of bed at 7:00 a.m. and fixed breakfast for herself and Clara. After finishing breakfast, Amber instructed Clara to go outside and play while she cleaned up the kitchen and did the day's laundry. While Clara was outside, Amber went into her bedroom and pulled a .45-caliber pistol out from underneath her bed. Checking the gun, Amber walked into James's bedroom. After making sure that he was still asleep, Amber raised the gun and fired two shots at James's head. *Bam! Bam!* Amber calmly walked over to the bed to make sure that James was dead. He was! Returning to her room, Amber placed the pistol back under the bed and went outside. Amber took Clara and fled to a neighbor's house where she called the Belfast police.

The Law Enforcement Investigation

Police officers with the Belfast Police Department arrived at the Cummings residence within fifteen minutes. Amber met them in her front yard and advised them that she had shot her husband, James. Amber directed them to the master bedroom where the body was located. The officers ascertained that James was dead and contacted police headquarters, requesting assistance from the coroner's office. While waiting on the coroner's office to arrive, the officer took a statement from Amber about the circumstances that led up to the shooting. Amber freely admitted that James had beaten her on several occasions and that she shot him, being in fear that he was going to beat her up again that day. Securing the crime scene, the officers located the .45-caliber pistol that had been the murder weapon and placed it in an evidence bag. The police chief of the Belfast Police Department arrived at the crime scene and advised the officers to take her to the police station for further interrogation.

Police Chief Jeffrey Trafton conducted a search of the crime scene while waiting on the coroner's office to arrive. During his search of the house, Chief Trafton was shocked to see a large collection of material related to Adolf Hitler and the Nazi Germany regime of the 1930s and 1940s. Searching the basement area of the house, Chief Trafton uncovered several containers which were filled with some sort of liquid materials. After conferring with several members of his department, Chief Trafton called the FBI and asked for a chemical weapons expert be sent to the crime scene.

Agents with the FBI office in Boston arrived at the Cummings residence on the afternoon of December 9, 2008. The agents examined the liquid containers and concluded that the items should be secured and transported to the FBI lab in Washington, DC, for further analysis. The FBI lab analysis indicated that the four jars contained depleted "Uranium-238," a chemical material that can be used to construct a "dirty bomb"! Other materials in the house were items that could be used to construct an "explosive device." Confiscating James's computer and electronic devices, the FBI analyst uncovered numerous Internet searches on methods that could be used to construct an "explosive bomb"! Further evidence on James's computer indicated that he had been searching areas in the area of the White House in which to place his "home-made dirty bomb." James apparently intended to construct the device, transport it to Washington hidden underneath the floor of his motorhome, and plant it in a strategic place along the inauguration route where President Obama would travel after being sworn into office. The FBI office turned over its final report to the Department of Homeland Security for a follow-up investigation. The final report with regard to the actions of James Cummings leading up to the date of his death had been classified as "top secret" and had not been released for public inspection. The Belfast Police Department concluded its investigation into the homicide of James Cummings and turned its report over to the office of the attorney general for the state of Maine. Amber dimming was arrested and subsequently charged with the crime of first-degree murder.

The Murder Trial of Amber Cummings

Amber Cummings was arraigned in the district court of Maine in the city of Belfast and entered a plea of "not guilty" to the charge of first-degree murder in the death of her husband. Prominent criminal defense attorney Eric Morse was selected to defend Amber on the murder charge. The state prosecutor selected to handle the prosecution was Assistant Attorney General Leana Zania. Several weeks later, a preliminary hearing was held in the case of *State of Maine v. Amber Cummings.*

During the hearing, the state presented the testimony of officers of the Belfast Police Department, including Police Chief Jeffrey Trafton. The officers testified that upon arriving at the residence on the morning of December 9, 2008, Mrs. Cummings met them in the front yard of the home and directed them to go inside the house and look inside the master bedroom. Inside there, the officers did find the body of James!

The officers testified about the crime scene and that they found the murder weapon in Amber's bedroom. Chief Trafton testified about his findings at the crime scene including a large stash of guns, knives, and other weapons in the closet of James's bedroom. Chief Trafton concluded his testimony discussing the large stash of chemical containers located in a room adjacent to James's bedroom. A representative of the coroner's office testified that the cause of death of James Cummings was the result of two gunshots wounds to the back of his head. Death was instantaneous! At the conclusion of the hearing, Amber Cummings was bound over for trial on the charge of first-degree murder. During the ensuing months, pretrial discovery was conducted.

During the pretrial discovery process, Amber's defense counsel requested that Amber be examined by a psychiatrist to determine the status of her mental health. The doctor selected to do the evaluation and spent more than twenty hours over several days doing a mental assessment of Amber before and after the date of the murder, December 9, 2008. At the conclusion of the evaluation process, the doctor issued a lengthy report, stating that in his professional opinion, Amber was "an abused wife" who suffered from a condition identified as the "battered women's syndrome." In his opinion, Amber could not escape the horrible living conditions associated with James's continuing mental and physical abuse. The doctor stated that on December 9, Amber "snapped" and decided that the only avenue of escape was for her to kill James while he was asleep. Upon receiving a copy of the report, the state's attorney requested an "independent evaluation" be conducted by a psychiatrist chosen by the state.

The court agreed and allowed the prosecutor to have Amber evaluated by its chosen doctor. A few weeks later, the doctor employed by the state furnished his report to the court relative to the mental evaluation of Amber Cummings. The report was shocking! The state's doctor disagreed with the defense doctor's evaluation. Amber Cummings was suffering from a neurological condition that caused her to be "a neurotic woman." The trial court ordered a third doctor to evaluate Amber's mental health. The report of the third doctor agreed with the evaluation of the doctor employed by the defense counsel and disagreed with the state's doctor! The court-appointed doctor concluded that Amber Cummings was seriously "mentally ill" at the time of the murder. The defense counsel contended that Amber could not go to a jury trial. The defense counsel decided to waive the defendant's right to a jury trial and have a nonjury trial before District Judge Jeffrey Hjelm.

On January 8, 2010, the trial of Amber Cummings was convened in the district court of Maine. Judge Jeffrey Hjelm was assigned as the judge to preside over the nonjury trial. The state's attorney again presented the testimony of members of the Belfast Police Department with regard to their investigation in the case. The prosecution emphasized that Amber had confessed twice to the killing her husband, James, on the morning on December 9, 2008: once at the crime scene when the police responded to the 911 call and a second time at the police station, during a follow-up interrogation at the police station. The state's attorney concluded the state's case by arguing that the only issue remaining to be decided by the judge was the punishment to be given to Amber Cummings. The state recommended that Amber be sentenced to serve a term of "*eight years*" in prison for the "cold-blooded" murder of James Cummings.

The defense counsel, Eric Morse, admitted that Amber shot and killed her husband, James, on the morning of December 9, 2008. However, Morse argued that there were extensive "extenuating circumstances" that the court needed to consider in making its decision. Attorney Morse presented the mental evaluation reports from two different psychiatrists that indicated that Amber suffered from a severe "mental impairment": the "battered women's syndrome"!

Morse contended that the continuing mental and physical abuse by James over a period of several years was the primary factor that caused Amber to "snap" and shoot James while he was asleep in bed on that December morning. At the conclusion of the defense case, the judge stated that he would recess the court hearing and reconvene court at 2:00 p.m. that day to announce his decision.

On the afternoon of January 8, 2010, Judge Jeffrey Hjelm reconvened court in the case of Amber Cummings to announce his decision. Judge Hjelm stated that there several factors that he considered in determining the appropriate punishment for Amber. These factors included the following:

1. The Cummings marriage was a very troubled marriage and that James Cummings was an "abusive husband" for many years. James had physically assaulted Amber on a daily basis during that period of time. As a result of that abuse, Amber was mentally ill on the date of the homicide, suffering a condition that the doctors identified as "the battered women's syndrome."
2. James was an abusive parent who would physically assault his daughter, Clara, on a regular basis.
3. James had an addiction to "child pornography," and he forced Amber to watch "child pornography" as a prelude to "sexual relations" between the couple.
4. James had possession of several dozen guns, swords, and other dangerous weapons; that James had possession of "bomb-making" materials that he intended to use to construct a "dirty bomb" to be used at a public event. James had bragged to two repairmen working at the Cummings house that he was going to "blow up" the president. Based on all these factors, James Cummings posed a serious continuing threat to Amber, Clara, and the rest of society.

Considering all these factors, Judge Hjelm pronounced his sentence. Amber Cummings was sentenced to *eight years*, with entire *eight* years to be *suspended* upon her good behavior. Amber Cummings walked out of the courthouse, a free woman at last! Amber and her daughter have lived a "quiet life" in seclusion for the past several years.

Analysis of the Amber Cummings Case

The facts of the Cummings case are shocking! How could James, a nice quiet young man in high school, turn into a domestic terrorist? The answer is simple: money!

When James inherited all the funds from a ten million trust set up by his father, James's character and personality changed dramatically! James evolved from a polite quiet young man to a living monster! The breaking point came when James became obsessed with bombs, acts of violence against the government, and "child pornography." James posed a serious threat to Amber and their daughter, Clara. Amber just did what any mother would do under similar circumstances to protect their child and themselves. Just kill him, and end the nightmare! The trial judge got it right. Amber should *not* go to jail for killing a monster, James Cummings!

A DEADLY CONFRONTATION
Virginia v. Breanna Sullivan (2018)

Breanna Sullivan was an outgoing, energetic young lady growing up in the Virginia Beach area of Virginia. She had a very active social life, dating several young men while attending high school. Breanna met Antonio Sullivan at a dance club one Saturday evening and was immediately impressed with his ability to sing and dance at the club. Breanna and Antonio started dating when she was sixteen years old. Wanting to escape her depressing home life, Breanna gladly accepted Antonio's invitation to share an apartment after finishing high school. Within a few months, Breanna learned that she was pregnant. Breanna gave birth to a beautiful baby girl whom the couple decided to name Kathy. Breanna got a job, working as a receptionist at a local insurance agency. While Breanna had a good steady job, Antonio had difficulty holding down a steady job. Things would go well for a few weeks, and then Antonio would get terminated for some "vague" reason. Antonio did not have a quality education, having dropped out of high school during the tenth grade. Antonio's employment was limited to jobs involving manual labor. With the couple dependent on Breanna's job as the main source of income, the romance that once existed between the couple disintegrated into constant fighting over money issues. Antonio would be gone several hours a day, supposedly out looking for a job. In truth, Antonio was out drinking with his friends and did very little in the way of searching for a good job. Breanna become increasingly suspicious that Antonio was seeing another woman. Confrontations between the couple would always end with physical violence. One day, Breanna shot and killed Antonio!

A History of Violence

The relationship between Breanna and Antonio was a very turbulent and uncertain during their five years together. It was great when both of them had a job and equally contributed to their joint-living expenses. However, when Antonio was out of work and looking for a job, the tension would continue to increase between the two of them. When Breanna would question Antonio about finding a job, he would got upset and start yelling at her. On March 30, 2015, Breanna called the police and asked for an officer to be dispatched to their apartment. When the officer arrived a few minutes later, Breanna signed a "citizen's complaint" to file assault and battery charges against Antonio. Police arrested Antonio and took him to the Virginia Beach Municipal Detention Center. Antonio was detained for three days, released only after he posted bond on the misdemeanor charge. Antonio was fined the sum of $300 and placed on probation for six months. Breanna and Antonio eventually reconciled and started living together again. The relationship was fine for a few months. On February 11, 2016, Breanna came home from work and found a woman naked in bed with Antonio. The woman grabbed her clothes and fled the apartment. Breanna and Antonio started fighting, and Antonio hit her in the head with a lamp, knocking her to the floor. Breanna was knocked unconscious and taken to a local hospital for treatment. The emergency room doctor diagnosed that Breanna had a "brain concussion" as a result of the blow to her head. Antonio was arrested and charged with "domestic battery." The couple reconciled after Antonio agreed to a "spousal counseling program" as a part of his probation. Breanna and Antonio reconciled eventually. A few months later, another fight ensued between the couple. Antonio threw Breanna on the floor and put a knife to her throat, telling her that he was going to kill her the next time that they had a fight. Breanna eventually was able to get up and go stay with her mother for a few days. During this period of time, Breanna bought a 9 mm handgun!

The Day of the Murder (July 16, 2017)

Breanna and Antonio eventually reconciled like they had done several times before.

Breanna had an appointment to go out to dinner with one of her friends from work on July 16, 2017. Antonio had agreed earlier in the day to be home by 5:00 that afternoon to watch their daughter so that Breanna could go out. Antonio finally showed up 6:30.

Breanna and Antonio started arguing over his failure to get home in a timely manner. Antonio became very upset and approached Breanna with his right hand raised in a clutched position, saying, "I am going to kill you!" Breanna reached in her handbag and pulled out her 9 mm pistol. Breanna yelled, "No, you are not!" Pointing her pistol directly at Antonio, she pulled the trigger. *Bam! Bam!* Antonio fell to the floor and was rendered unconscious. Breanna picked up her cellphone and dialed 911 for the Virginia Beach Police Department. An ambulance and the police arrived within fifteen minutes. Antonio was transported to a Virginia Beach hospital. The emergency room doctor pronounced Antonio Sullivan dead an hour later. Breanna admitted that she shot and killed Antonio after he came at her and threatened to kill her. The Virginia Beach police arrested Breanna and transported her to jail. Once Breanna got to the police station, she was interrogated by police detectives and eventually signed a confession, freely admitting that she shot Antonio after he threatened to beat her up again. Breanna related to the police that she had been the victim of three prior assaults by Antonio and that she had had "enough!" Virginia Department of Human Services was summoned to take temporary custody of Breanna's daughter. The daughter was later turned over to Breanna's sister during the court proceedings.

Virginia v. Breanna Sullivan (2017)

Breanna Sullivan was arraigned on a charge of second-degree murder in a Virginia court on July 18, 2017. Breanna entered a plea of "*not guilty*" and requested a jury trial. Bond was denied since the charge was murder. Another hearing was scheduled for July 25, 2017.

The court, after hearing evidence about the circumstances of the homicide, ordered the state's attorney to reduce the charge down to first-degree manslaughter. The defendant, after consulting with her attorney, waived her right to a jury trial and asked the court to set the case for a nonjury trial. The Circuit Court of Virginia conducted a non-jury trial for Breanna Sullivan in December 3rd, 2018. The state called several law enforcement officers that testified that Breanna Sullivan admitted shooting Antonio Sullivan twice when they got into a domestic quarrel on the evening of July 16, 2017. A representative of the Virginia State coroner's office testified that the death of Antonio Sullivan was caused by two gunshots, fired at close range, to the face and neck. The prosecution rested its case.

The counsel for the defense, James Broccoletti, presented certified court records of all the criminal charges that had been filed against Antonio Sullivan for the past five years. The records revealed that Sullivan had been charged with "assault and battery," "domestic battery," and "assault with a deadly weapon" during the marriage. In addition, the Virginia courts had issued three different "protective orders" for Breanna Sullivan in connection with the criminal charges. Additional testimony was presented by several witnesses indicating that Breanna had been treated by medical care providers on several occasions after being assaulted by Antonio. Witnesses from Breanna's place of employment testified that she frequently showed up at work with contusions and bruises on her face and arms.

Virginia v. Breanna Sullivan Trial (Continued)

Breanna Sullivan took the witness stand and testified in her own defense. Breanna described in detail her five-year relationship with Antonio Sullivan. She said that the marriage was great at first. Antonio was a great person with an outstanding personality. However, within a few months, Antonio exhibited a totally different personality. Antonio became increasingly abusive and violent. The couple would have "domestic disputes" that generally ended when he assaulted her and threatened to kill her. Breanna admitted that she had a "kind and forgiving heart" and that they reconcile within a few weeks. Breanna admitted that she purchased a 9 mm pistol after being assaulted by Antonio on a prior occasion. She also admitted that she pulled the pistol out of her handbag and shot Antonio on the evening of July 16, 2017, after he punched her and knocked her to the floor. The defense rested its case and submitted the case to the court for its decision.

The Verdict of the Court

On December 5, 2018, the district court of Virginia, Circuit Court Judge A. B. Shockley reconvened to announce the court's decision. Judge Shockley, reciting the testimony from the witnesses and the court records, concluded that Breanna Sullivan was "*not guilty*" of the crime of voluntary manslaughter. Breanna's was released from custody and allowed to go home. Free at last after eighteen months in a "legal nightmare." Breanna was eventually allowed to regain custody of her daughter and return to a normal life.

Analysis of the Breanna Sullivan Case

The Breanna Sullivan case is a good example of the growing trend of the American legal system to recognize the right of woman to use "deadly force" when they are the "victim" of continuing domestic violence. Breanna had suffered through almost five years of domestic violence at the hands of her husband, Antonio Sullivan. The Circuit Court of Virginia, Judge A. B. Shockley, noted in her findings the following factors that influenced her decision:

1. Antonio Sullivan had a long history of violence toward his wife, Breanna Sullivan. Antonio had been charged, on three separate occasions, with assault and battery, domestic battery, and assault with a deadly weapon.
2. Judge Shockley noted, in issuing her opinion, that during these three assaults, Breanna had sustained physical injuries that required medical treatment for her injuries at nearby medical facilities.

3. The Virginia courts had, on three separate occasions, issued "protective orders" for Breanna Sullivan, prohibiting Antonio from being around Breanna and her daughter, Kathy. These orders were later withdrawn at the request of Breanna after the couple eventually reconciled and got back together.

4. The judge concluded that Breanna was a good example of the "battered women's syndrome," feeling that her only way out of her "domestic nightmare" she was living was to end the marriage. Breanna did just that when she pulled out her 9 mm pistol and killed Antonio Sullivan on July 17, 2017!

THE DEATH OF AN
EX-HUSBAND
Florida v. Cara Ryan (2015)

Cara Ryan was born in Florida in the 1970s. Growing up in the "sunshine state," Cara enjoyed the warm climate and the sunny beaches. During high school, Cara dreamed of a job where she could have time off during the summer months to enjoy the climate and many of Florida's sunny beaches. Cara also developed a passion for journalism. Realizing that the perfect way to pursue her career in journalism and have lots of time for summer at the beach, Cara settled on the idea of being a teacher, a high school journalism teacher! That type of deal would allow her to enjoy both the climate and the working conditions. Cara enrolled in college. After graduation, Cara applied for a teaching position at several area high schools and was granted an interview with a high school in Clearwater, Florida. Cara did a great job during the interview and was hired as the journalism teacher for Clearwater High School.

Cara enjoyed her job immensely and became one of the most respected teachers at Clearwater High School. Having accomplished her primary goal in life, Cara turned her focus to finding the perfect husband! A difficult task for any woman! Especially Cara! She considered herself a very "independent" woman.

John Rush was born in Florida in the late 1960s. Growing up, John aspired to work in law enforcement. John wanted to be a "police officer." After finishing his public education, John entered a police officer training program certified by the state of the Florida Department of Public Safety. After completion of the program, John applied for a position as a police officer at several large municipal government entities across the state of Florida. John was invited to an interview with the St. Petersburg Police Department. Great interview! John was hired immediately!

Cara Ryan focused on her teaching career the first few years while she worked at Clearwater High School. While Cara dated during this period, she never found anyone who wanted a permanent relationship. However, that all changed one day when she had a uniformed police officer come into her journalism class to talk about community relations between the press and law enforcement. The St. Petersburg Police Department assigned a uniformed officer to go to speak to Cara's class. His name was John "JJ" Rush! Rush made a great presentation! The couple hit it off and started dating. Cara learned that JJ had recently gone through a difficult divorce and had a young daughter named Meghan. Within a few months, Cara sensed that JJ was the perfect man for her. Cara and JJ were married in 1996 and enjoyed a "honeymoon" in the Caribbean! With both of them having secure government jobs, the couple was able to buy the home of their dreams, in Indian Rocks Beach community. The house was located within a hundred yards of the beach.

During the first few years of their marriage, things were great between Cara and JJ Rush. Cara was busy with her teaching career, earning the top honor as "Teacher of the Year" at Clearwater High School. Likewise, JJ was busy in his duties with the St. Petersburg Police Department, working in the patrol division and later in the crime scene investigation unit.

JJ was promoted to the rank of sergeant in 1998. While the couple discussed the idea of having children, the demands of their careers made it difficult to finalize their plans. Cara was very happy serving as a stepmother to Meghan, JJ's daughter from his first marriage. Tragedy struck the couple in 2005 when JJ was involved in a motor vehicle accident while on duty with the police department. The car was "totaled out," and JJ suffered severe injuries to his neck and back. JJ was off work and under doctor's care for several months. After many months of physical therapy, the doctors concluded that

JJ was permanently disabled to the extent that he could not return to his duties as a police officer. JJ was forced to retire in 2005.

Cara became the primary breadwinner with JJ's retirement. While JJ received a retired officer's pay, Cara was forced to make the house payment, car payments, and their utility bills at home. A change in lifestyles for the couple who had previously enjoyed a life of luxury. JJ had trouble coping with injuries from the auto accident and turned to "painkiller pills" and liquor to help relieve his discomfort. The pain medications, including "oxycodone" became quite addictive to JJ and he had trouble sleeping. Unable to sleep at night, JJ started drinking hard liquor in order to get to sleep. JJ's behavior became more irrational as time wore on. The stress of the drugs and drinking had an impact on their marriage. The breaking point came when JJ flew into a rage one evening and struck Cara, knocking her to the floor. Within weeks, Cara filed for divorce in Pinellas County. After months of legal wrangling, the couple agreed on the terms of the divorce, and the court entered a decree of divorce in 2005. JJ sought treatment for his alcohol and drug issues. JJ was also able to get a new job with the Pinellas County Medical Examiner's Office. With his personal problems now resolved, JJ asked Cara to reconsider their relationship. Cara agreed to the reconciliation as long as JJ continued his rehabilitation program. JJ moved back into Cara's house in 2006, and it seemed like "old times" for a few months. Eventually, JJ returned to his old habits of drinking and using painkillers. During their separation, JJ acquired a new hobby: going to casinos and getting drunk.

Cara was once again faced with a difficult decision. What should she do with her ex-husband? Cara forced him to move out of her home and get his own apartment. During the next few years, Cara and JJ experienced an "on and off" relationship. While Cara managed their finances, JJ was forced to live own his own. JJ would come and go from her house, staying a few days with her and staying in his own apartment the rest of the week. Eventually, Cara got tired of the arrangement and started considering the possibility of seeing other men. JJ also started to move on, looking for another woman.

The Day of the Murder (March 7, 2015)

Cara and JJ had not seen each other for several weeks. Cara felt all alone in the world. On the evening of March 7, she sent JJ a text, asking if he could stop by and see her for a few minutes.

JJ texted back, telling Cara that he would be over later that evening. At approximately 9:00 p.m., Cara was watching television when JJ arrived. She invited him in for a few minutes. The couple was talking for about thirty minutes when Cara excused herself. Cara came back in the room a few minutes later dressed in a very revealing see-through nightgown. The couple retired to the bedroom and enjoyed a few minutes of "intimate" privacy. Cara got up out of bed and went to the restroom. JJ glanced over to the nightstand and saw Cara's cellphone on the table. Reaching for it, JJ glanced through it and saw that Cara had sent a very intimate text to another number. JJ become quite upset and jumped out of bed. Throwing his clothes on, JJ yelled at Cara, telling her that he was leaving. Coming out of the bathroom, Cara was shocked to see JJ leaving the house in a hurry. She wondered what had happened. Glancing down at her cellphone, she noticed that it had been moved. Instantly, Cara realized what had happened. JJ had gone through her cellphone and saw the text that she had sent earlier that evening to another male friend of hers. Cara collapsed onto the bed, realizing that a good evening had been ruined by her own stupidity: leaving her phone out where JJ could see it. Cara checked the door to make sure it was locked and took a sleeping pill, hoping to get some sleep. Turning out the lights, Cara retired to the bedroom. A few minutes later, Cara thought she heard a noise coming from the area of the patio. Reaching into her nightstand next to the bed, Cara pulled out her gun, a .38-caliber pistol that JJ had given her several years earlier. Cara saw a dark figure entering her bedroom. Raising the gun, Cara pulled the trigger. *Bam!*

The bullet went astray and missed the intended target. The intruder, a large man, knocked the gun out of her hand and jumped into the bed, landing on top of her. Cara instantly recognized that the intruder was her ex-husband! JJ started yelling at her, telling her that he was going to "bust her open" and "that no man would ever want her again"! Ripping her robe off, JJ pinned Cara down on the bed and sexually assaulted her. The "nightmare ordeal" went on for more than thirty minutes. Getting up, JJ told Cara that the next time that he saw her, he was "going to kill her!" JJ pulled his clothes back on and started to leave the room. Seeing the gun lying in the floor next to the bed, Cara picked it up and yelled, "Take this, you bastard!" Cara pulled the trigger on the gun. *Bam!* The bullet struck JJ in the arm and penetrated his chest. JJ stumbled out of the room and left the house. Collapsing back into her bed, Cara reflected on what had just happened at her house. After a few moments of reflection, Cara decided to call the police and report the shooting incident.

Cara dialed 911 for the local police department. Cara advised the operator that an intruder had entered her house and that she fired her gun at him. Cara told the operator that she thought the burglar was wounded and that he had fled the crime scene. Approximately, twenty minutes later, officers with the Clearwater Police Department arrived at the scene. Cara met the officers in her driveway and told them what had just happened. Cara was detained and placed in the back of a police car. Two police officers went inside the house to inspect the crime scene. The officers were later joined by deputies with the Pinellas County Sheriff's Office. The body of JJ Rush was found on the patio of a neighbor's house adjacent to Cara's house. The detectives determined that he was dead! The body of JJ Rush was removed from the scene and transported to the Pinellas County coroner's office for an autopsy. Cara was arrested and taken to the Pinellas County Sheriff's Office for further interrogation. After ten hours of interrogation, Cara was released. A few days later, Cara was charged with murder!

The Court Proceedings

On March 10, 2007, Cara Ryan was arraigned in the district court of Pinellas County, state of Florida, on a charge of first-degree murder. Cara entered a plea of "not guilty" and exercised her legal right to a jury trial on the charge. The court ordered that the case be set for a jury trial on the next available docket. Cara selected Roger

Futerman, a well-known criminal defense lawyer, to defend her. The defense filed a motion to allow the defendant to be released from jail, contending that the evidence did not support a charge of first-degree murder. At the hearing, the judge agreed, ruling the charge be amended to a charge of second-degree murder.

Cara was ordered released on a bond of $250,000. Cara was able to post the required bond within a few hours, and she was released from jail. A few weeks later, a show-cause hearing was conducted in Cara's case. The court ruled that there was sufficient evidence to order the case to trial. The case was continued for several months due to the crowded Florida court dockets. During the ensuing months, Defense Attorney Futerman filed several motions for production of evidence relative to all the documents and reports that the law enforcement authorities had received during their investigation in the homicide. More than three hundred pages of documents and reports were turned over to the defense counsel. One of the most interesting pieces of evidence released was the videotaped statements that Cara had given to the police at the police station on the evening of the shooting. Reviewing the videos and related documents, Futerman noted that Cara had been subjected to more than ten hours of intense interrogation, lasting all through the night and into the following morning. During all these hours of questioning, Cara was confined to one room and was not allowed to have the assistance of an attorney. The defense counsel had to determine whether Cara had given a Miranda rights waiver.

The defense counsel filed a "motion to suppress" the statements that Cara had given at the police station, contending that the statements and confession were "coerced" from Cara. A court hearing on the motion concluded that the Miranda rights warnings had been given to Cara twice: once in the police car at the crime scene and a second time at the police station during the interrogation. Other information uncovered during the discovery process included the medical records of JJ Rush. The medical records revealed that Rush was actively taking prescriptions for oxycodone and Xanax. The autopsy report did not show any positive results with regard to alcohol or drugs. The most startling piece of evidence uncovered was that law enforcement had obtained a search warrant to examine and preserve the Facebook records that Cara had used following the shooting. The records revealed that Cara had contacted several people with regard to whether those people would be favorable witnesses for the defense in her case. Attorney Futerman had to determine whether Cara was trying to create evidence that supported her claim that Rush was an out-of-control drunk and drug addict.

After reviewing all the evidence, the defense counsel determined that the most important aspect of the trial would be how a jury would receive the evidence and determine the proper verdict to be given in the case. Attorney Futerman decided to conduct a "mock jury trial" and see what members of a jury would consider and what verdict would the "mock jury" render. During the "mock jury," Cara would testify to the events that occurred on the night of the shooting. At the conclusion of the "mock trial," the jury concluded that Cara was probably guilty and that she should be sent to prison for the rest of her life. At the conclusion of the process, the defense counsel noted that men on the "mock jury" were more sympathetic toward Cara. Attorney Futerman concluded that the "jury selection process" would be the most crucial part of the case. The case was finally set for a jury trial in January 2017.

The Jury Trial for Cara Ryan

In January 2017, the jury trial for Cara Ryan was conducted in the district court of Pinellas County, Florida. During the jury selection process, the defense counsel pursed the idea that male jurors would be the best persons to be on the jury. Defense Attorney Futerman also wanted to find jurors who owned a home and also possessed a gun. Finally, the jury was seated in the case. The panel consisted of five men and one woman. All the jurors were homeowners who believed in an individual's rights under the Second Amendment. Since the burden of proof in a criminal case is on the prosecution, the Florida District Attorney's Office went first in the case. The state called several members of the Pinellas County Sheriff's Office and the local police department to present their testimony in the case. The state's evidence related the findings of the officers when they arrived at the crime scene. The extensive videotaped statements given by Cara at the police station were also played for the jury. The coroner's office presented evidence about the autopsy results, indicating that the death of victim, JJ Rush, was caused by "blunt-force trauma," a single gunshot wound to the chest that penetrated the heart. At the conclusion of the state's evidence, the prosecutor rested his case.

Defense counsel Futerman presented testimony about the medical history of JJ Rush, placing emphasis on the fact that the victim had permanent injuries related his automobile accident from 2005 and that he took several prescriptions including oxycodone and Xanax. Evidence was also presented that Rush had a "heavy drinker" who indulged in alcohol to relieve the tremendous pain that he experienced due to the injuries. The biggest problem that defense counsel had to decide: whether Cara should take the stand and testify in her own defense.

Cara Ryan decided to testify and took the witness stand to present her testimony on the morning of January 22, 2017. Cara stated that she was married to JJ Rush for nine years. That JJ was a good husband for the first few years of her marriage. That all changed after JJ suffered severe injuries in an automobile accident while working for the police department in 2005. Cara stated that her husband was in constant pain as a result of his head and back injuries and that he was forced to take high-powered pain-relief medicines including oxycodone. The drugs changed his personality, and he became increasingly abusive and violent. Cara stated that she feared for her own personal safety and that she was forced to file for a divorce and get a "protective order" against JJ Rush. Cara stated that the divorce was finalized in 2006. Following several months of drug rehabilitation, JJ asked for a second chance. Cara stated that she still loved JJ and that she decided to give him a second chance. Cara stated that although JJ had his own place, he would stay at Cara's house for several days each week. Cara testified that JJ eventually returned to his old habits of taking excessive amounts of drugs and getting drunk several times per week. Cara decided that she had had enough at this point and that she told JJ to leave and "not come back around!" Cara stated that they had been separated for several weeks when she sent him a text on March 7, 2015, inquiring as to how he was doing. JJ replied, asking Cara if he could come over and see her. Cara agreed. Cara stated that JJ showed up about 9:00 p.m. and that they talked and retired to the bedroom to enjoy some "intimate privacy." Cara got up and went to the bathroom. JJ became enraged after going through her cellphone and finding an intimate message to another man. Cara stated that JJ left the house. He came back about thirty minutes later and brutally assaulted her. Cara retrieved her gun and shot JJ as he was leaving the bedroom.

After spending several hours on the witness stand, Cara was excused as a witness, and the defense rested its case. The judge and attorneys retired to the judge's chambers to review the proper instructions that should be given to the jury. The defense presented the argument that the jury should be given an instruction on the right of "self-defense" since Cara was in her own home at the time of the shooting. The judge agreed, despite the objections of the state's attorney. Returning to the courtroom, the judge gave the jury instructions on the burden of proof, the credibility of the witnesses, and the right of the defense to assert use of "self-defense." Attorneys for both sides presented closing arguments to the jury panel composed of five men and one woman. The jury retired and began its deliberations.

The Jury Verdict

The jury deliberated for approximately ninety minutes and arrived at a verdict. All parties: the judge, the prosecutor, and the defense counsel were shocked at the quick jury verdict. The jury returned to the courtroom, and the judge announced the verdict. The unanimous verdict of the jury was "*not guilty*"! The judge excused the jury and directed the clerk to record the verdict. The judge ordered that Cara be released and that her bond be exonerated. Cara walked out of the courtroom, at last a "free woman" after two years of legal uncertainty. A poll of the jury panel, upon leaving the courtroom, indicated that it was clearly a case of "self-defense." JJ daughter, Meghan, filed a wrongful death against Cara. That action was dismissed by the Pinellas County court in 2019.

Analysis of the Cara Ryan Case

The criminal prosecution of Cara Ryan was seriously flawed in many respects. The basic facts indicate that JJ Rush was shot and killed inside the residence of Cara Ryan on the evening of March 7, 2015. When the police arrived, they placed Cara Ryan in handcuffs and left her in a police car for more than three hours. Cara told the responding officers that she had been brutally assaulted and raped in her own bedroom by the victim, JJ Rush. Did the police take her to a medical facility to be checked out by medical personnel after being the victim of a sexual assault? *No!* Cara Ryan was transported to the police station for further interrogation. She was held in custody for more than ten hours before finally being released at 8:00 a.m. the next day. Why was a law-abiding citizen treated in such an outrageous manner? Consider these possible factors:

1. The victim, JJ Rush, was a retired police officer who was known and respected among the law enforcement community; law enforcement tried desperately to make the case look like of "a cold-blooded murder" instead of a case that was clearly "justifiable homicide."

2. The actual victim was Cara Ryan. Cara should have taken to the hospital immediately for a physical exam to determine whether she was the victim of a sexual assault. Photographs taken of Cara after the incident clearly showed that Cara had bruises and contusions on her arms and wrists. The prosecutor claimed that the bruises resulted from being handcuffed for more than four hours.

3. After Cara was arrested, she was held on charge of first-degree murder! This type of charge was wrong. The judge determined that considering all the facts, the proper charge was one of second-degree murder and ordered that the

charge be amended and Cara released after posting the required amount of bond.

4. The defense counsel for Cara Ryan presented testimony and medical records of the victim, JJ Rush, that indicated that he was taking heavy doses of oxycodone and Xanax for pain that resulted from the disabling injuries that he sustained from a wreck involving his police car when he was on active duty. These drugs are highly addictive and can cause serious mental health issues if taken over a long period of time. In contrast to these known facts, the autopsy report found no evidence of traces of the drugs in his remains! How interesting is that fact? Was the autopsy report accurate? Remember that the victim worked for that same office prior to his death! A coincidence!

5. The crime scene was inside Cara Ryan's house. The common-law rule is that a homeowner has the right to "use deadly force" if they are faced with a threat that they are in "imminent danger" caused by the sudden appearance of an intruder. Cara had the absolute legal right to shoot JJ Rush when he came into her house and brutally assaulted her. The police and the prosecutor totally ignored the legal standard rule in Florida that Cara properly exercised her legal right of self-defense.

Conclusion

The case of the *State of Florida v. Cara Ryan* should have never been filed, based on the facts presented and the law of the state of Florida. It was clearly a case of justifiable homicide!

DEADLY DISPUTE
Missouri v. Ashley Hunter (2015)

Ashley Hunter was born in Warren County, Missouri, in 1988. Ashley got married to her high school sweetheart when she was only eighteen years of age. She had her first child when she was twenty. Enjoying being a mother, Ashley had her second child when she was twenty-three. After her husband left her for another woman, Ashley felt lost and without a man in her life. Raising two kids as a single parent is a difficult task for any woman. Things would change. In 2013, Ashley meet Nicholas, and the pair started dating.

Within one year, Nicholas asked Ashley to marry him. Nicholas appeared to be a good prospect for a husband. Nick was a licensed electrician working for a heating and air company outside of St. Louis, Missouri. The marriage that appeared to be made in heaven turned out to be "a living nightmare" within a few months.

There were constant heated arguments between Ashley and Nicholas over issues related to money. Nicholas was paying considerable child support to his ex-wife for the support of his two children from a prior marriage. This put a financial strain on Ashley's marriage. Since Ashley had two children of her own, the couple was having financial issues on both sides. While Nicholas made good money working as an electrician, there never seemed to be enough money to cover the couple's monthly living expenses. The financial problems in the marriage caused Nicholas to start drinking. Evenings generally ended with Nicholas downing ten cans of beer. Ashley Hunter's "honeymoon" marriage turned into "a living nightmare" in a few months.

The Day of the Murder (January, 15, 2015)

Nicholas Hunter was a licensed electrician working for a large heating and air-conditioning company in St. Louis, Missouri. During the winter months, Nicholas would work twelve hours days, answering service calls to repair heating systems in the area. Nick would frequently leave for work at 7:00 a.m. and not get home till 9:00 p.m. The money was needed to take care of the couple's monthly living expenses. On January 15, 2015, Nick left for work shortly after 7:00. Ashley saw him off to work. After dropping her daughter off at school, Ashley drove over to visit with her mother. Since her mother was not feeling well, Ashley agreed to go buy her groceries for the week. Ashley returned to her mother's house and dropped off her groceries. Ashley returned home in the afternoon. Ashley was surprised to see Nicholas's vehicle in the driveway when she returned home. Upon entering the house, Ashley was confronted by Nick.

"Where have you been?" he asked.

Ashley replied, "I went over to visit my mom. She is under the weather, so I went to the grocery store for her."

Nick grabbed her as she entered the door. "I don't believe you! Where have you been? Out with one of your old boyfriends?"

"No," Ashley responded, pulling away from him. Walking to the kitchen, Ashley asked Nick, "Why are you home this time of the day? You generally don't get home before dark."

Grabbing another can of beer out of the icebox, Nick responded, "I have been fired!"

"Why?" she asked.

Sitting down on the sofa, Nick answered, "The boss said that I had too many customer complaints made against me!"

Ashley uttered, "I don't understand! I thought you were their best employee."

Slowly getting up from the sofa, Nick grabbed another beer out of the refrigerator. Gulping the beer down, Nick admitted, "They searched my service vehicle and found some syringes inside my truck! They think that I am taking some sort of steroids!"

Ashley stepped away in a total state of misbelief. Pausing for a moment, Ashley stated, "I knew that you were going to get caught, sooner or later! That does it. I am leaving."

Ashley walked out of the kitchen, opened the living room closet, and pulled out two suitcases. Nick grabbed Ashley and said, "No, you are not leaving me!"

Ashley pulled away and said, "Yes, I am. Let's face it! You are a loser! I am not going to stay married to another loser!"

Ashley pulled away, intent on packing and leaving the house. Nicholas grabbed Ashley and pulled her closer to him. Ashley struggled and finally got loose from him She headed into the bedroom to begin packing. Nicholas came into the bedroom and went to the closet. Reaching onto the top shelf, Nicholas pulled out a pistol and turned around, moving toward Ashley. Raising the gun, Nicholas pointed it at Ashley and said, "You are not leaving me, not now, not ever!"

Getting closer to Ashley, Nicholas pointed the gun at her head. Ashley kicked Nicholas between the legs, striking him in the area of his testicles. Momentarily stunned, Nicholas dropped the gun on the floor and winced in pain. Ashley grabbed the gun and pointed it at Nicholas. Pausing for a couple of seconds, Ashley squeezed the trigger. *Bam! Bam! Bam! Bam!* Nicholas fell to the floor, twisting in pain. Ashley fired the gun again, pumping four more shots into Nicholas as he was lying on the floor.

After checking on Nick, Ashley went to the phone and dialed 911. The sheriff's department of Warren County, Missouri, responded to the emergency call. Within twenty minutes, sheriff's deputies arrived at the residence on Cottonwood Road. Deputies entered the house and found Nicholas lying on the floor in the bedroom. An examination disclosed that Nicholas was dead. Deputies secured the crime scene and had the body removed from the residence and transported to the coroner's office. Ashley was escorted down to the sheriff's substation to give a formal statement.

Ashley was advised of her Miranda rights and signed a formal written waiver of her Miranda rights. Two detectives questioned Ashley for several hours and conferred with the district attorney's office. At the conclusion of the questioning, Ashley was released from custody and allowed to go to her mother's house to stay that evening.

After completing their investigation and obtaining the coroner's report on the cause of death, the Warren County sheriffs turned in their paperwork, recommending that felony charges be filed against Ashley Hunter. On January 22, 2015, Ashley was contacted by the Warren County Sheriff's Department and requested to come down to sheriff's office. Ashley, sensing that she was going to be arrested, took several Xanax pills to calm down. Getting into her car, Ashley drove down toward the sheriff's station. On the way to the station, Ashley was driving down Interstate 70 when she was involved in an accident. Emergency personnel transported Ashley to a nearby hospital. Sheriff's deputies arrested Ashley at the hospital and took her to jail. Ashley Hunter was charged with first-degree murder on January 23, 2015.

The Murder Trial for Ashley Hunter

Ashley Hunter appeared before the district court of Warren County, Missouri, and entered a plea of "*not guilty*," requesting a jury trial. Scott Rosenblum was selected to represent Ashley. The court ordered Ashley to post a bail bond in the amount of $1 million. Ashley was financially unable to post the bond and was remanded to the Warren County Jail until the date of the jury trial. *Four years* later, the criminal trial of Ashley finally came on for trial. The jury selection process resulted in a jury panel composed of seven men and five women. The state of Missouri prosecutor presented testimony from deputies of the Warren County Sheriff's Department related to the statements made by Ashley in the 911 call to the sheriff's office, the evidence collected at the crime scene, and the statements that Ashley gave at the sheriff's office. Evidence was also presented from the state medical examiner's office, indicating the Nicholas Hunter died as the result to eight gunshots wounds to the chest and back. During the defense presentation of evidence, it was disclosed that Nicholas was an abusive husband who was a heavy drinker and a drug abuser. Several syringes belonging to Nicholas were admitted into evidence.

Expert testimony from a chemist indicated that the syringes contained residue of steroid materials. The autopsy report also indicated that Nicholas was legally drunk with a high level of alcohol in his blood. Ashley took the witness stand, in her own defense, and described in detail to the abusive behavior she had suffered at the hands of her husband during their marriage of less than one year. On the date of the homicide, Ashley told Nicholas that she had had enough and that she was leaving him. Nicholas became enraged and grabbed Ashley and started choking her. During the struggle, Ashley managed to get loose and tried to leave. Nicholas grabbed a gun out of the closet and pointed it at Ashley's head. Ashley testified that she kicked him in the groin area. In immediate pain, Nicholas dropped the gun. Ashley related that she picked up the gun and instinctively fired it at Nicholas. Ashley could not remember how many shots were fired from the gun. Nicholas fell to the floor and slowly passed out. At the conclusion of her testimony, the trial judge gave the appropriate instructions to the jury and asked them to retire and begin their deliberations.

The Jury Verdict

The jury panel in the Ashley Hunter case was given several issues to deliberate and These issues include the following:

1. Was the killing of Nicholas Hunter an act of murder by the defendant, Ashley Hunter?
2. Was the homicide a crime of manslaughter considering the circumstances of spousal abuse?
3. Was the defendant, Ashley Hunter, entitled to claim the shooting was one of self-defense?

The jury panel, after several hours of deliberations, returned to open court and announced Their unanimous verdict to the court. The jury rendered a verdict of "*not guilty* on all *charges*." The trial court accepted the jury's verdict and ordered Ashley Hunter to be released from custody immediately.

Analysis of the Ashley Hunter Case

The jury verdict in the Ashley Hunter case obviously reflects the jury's view on the issue of whether a woman may use deadly force when she was the victim of spousal abuse by a husband. The victim, Nicholas Hunter, was an abusive husband who was drunk and pulled a gun, threatening to kill her. What other choice did Ashley have to protect herself from further physical abuse and bodily injury? Factors in the case that may have influenced the jury include the following:

1. Nicholas was an alcoholic who drank ten to twelve beers a day. The autopsy report indicated that he was totally drunk. His blood alcohol content was above the legal limit recognized as the standard to measure intoxication.
2. Nicholas was a drug addict. On the date of his death, he had been fired from his job after the supervisor found syringes in his work truck. The police also found syringes in the house when they searched the crime scene.
3. The jury panel was composed of an equal number of women and men (six women and six men). Since the jury verdict was unanimous, all members of the jury panel had to agree to enter a verdict of not guilty.

The big unresolved issue in the case, Why was Ashley Hunter held in jail for *four long years* on an extremely high bond ($1 million) waiting to have her day in court? That was *outrageous* considering the fact that the jury found her not guilty.

WHO KILLED JON GARNER
Texas v. Sandra Garner (2018)

On January 2, 2018, Sandra Garner, an East Texas housewife, was sound asleep in the bedroom of the large Texas home when she was awakened by the sounds of gunshots in the house. Two shots! *Bam! Bam!* The shots were fired from a gun that was very close to her bedroom. Sandra slowly opened her eyes to observe a tall stranger standing over her bed. The tall strange man, dressed in dark clothing, was wearing a mask covering his head and was holding a gun in his right hand.

"What the hell is going on?" she asked.

The stranger, in a harsh-sounding voice, said, "Relax, lady. I mean you no harm. I come here to pay back your husband for all the hell that he has caused in my life!"

"What do you mean?" she asked.

"I worked at the company where your husband was my boss. He fired me twelve months ago! I have lost my job, my wife, my family, and everything that means anything to me."

Sandra paused for a few seconds to let the words sink in. "The gunshots! What did you do to Jon?" she asked. The stranger motioned over to the floor of the bedroom on the other side of her bed. Sandra slowly peeked over the bed and was shocked to see her beloved husband, Jon, lying on the floor with blood all over the area on the floor next to his body. "Oh my God." She gasped as she slumped back in her bed.

A moment of silence was broken by the stranger. "Get up out of bed, lady! Show me where the money box is hidden," he demanded in a very commanding voice.

Sandra collected her senses and slowly got out of her bed. Standing upright, and clutching the bed cover around her body, she asked, "What do you want?"

"Where is the money?" he demanded.

"What money?" she asked.

"The cash box," he answered. "Where is it?"

Sandra looked puzzled by the question. "What are you talking about?"

The stranger, moving closer to the bed, demanded, "Quit stalling. Show me the money, now!"

"What money are you talking about?" she asked.

"Lady, I know your husband kept a small safe lockbox containing money here at the house! He used to brag about it at work! Now get it out here, and empty it on the bed here. Now! Or else I am going to use this on you." He waved the gun around that he held in his right hand. Sandra slowly moved toward the closet located on the far side of the bedroom. Opening the door, she flipped on the closet light. The intruder moved closer. "Careful now," he exclaimed. "I know that your husband kept several guns stashed in the house. He bragged about it at work!" Sandra reached in the closet and retrieved a small metal box that was locked. She carried it over to the bed and unlocked the box with a key that was on the nightstand next to the bed. Opening the box, she stepped back as the stranger grabbed the box and flipped it upside down, dumping the contents out on the bed. The stranger grabbed up the money and started shoving it into his coat pockets. "There is a lot of money in here. It has got to be more than $10,000. That's what he bragged about!" The intruder finished scooping up the cash and cramming into both of his coat pockets. Turning to leave, he said, "Don't do anything stupid, like calling the police! If you do, then I will come back and blow your head off!" The stranger turned and ran out of the front door of the house. Sandra slumped back into her bed and reflected on what had just happened. Sandra clutched her chest and jumped up and ran over to check on her husband, Jon. Blood was splattered all over the floor around his body. Realizing that he was still alive, Sandra grabbed the bedroom phone and dialed 911. After a couple of rings, the dispatcher, a woman, came on the line. "Nine, one, one emergency! What is your emergency?" Clutching the phone, Sandra replied, "Help, my husband has been shot! Send help now!"

The Police Investigation

The 911 call was made at 12:45 a.m. to the Maypearl, Texas Police Department. Law enforcement arrived at the Garner residence within thirty minutes. The responding officer took the offense report from Sandra Garner.

She described the suspect as a tall man who was probably in his late thirties who was wearing blue jeans, a dark-colored jacket, and a dark mask covering his face. The officer made a search of the crime scene and observed Jon Garner lying on the floor of the master bedroom. The officer determined that the victim was shot in the chest area. The officer requested emergency assistance from medical personnel and made a search of the premises to determine if the suspect was still in the area. While waiting on medical assistance, the officer took several pictures with his cell phone of the crime scene. Sandra lay down on the living room sofa, crying hysterically about what had just occurred. Paramedics arrived within a few minutes and attempted to revive the victim. Sandra was interviewed more extensively and subsequently taken to the local sheriff's office in Ellis County, Texas. Sandra was questioned thoroughly by local law enforcement. Sandra repeated the story about an unknown intruder who had entered the house and shot her husband. Sandra was finally released from custody and allowed to return home several hours later. An autopsy report from the Ellis County coroner's office revealed that Jon Garner suffered fatal injuries caused by two gunshots fired at close range. Law enforcement interviewed friends and relatives of the Garner family to ascertain "possible persons of interest" who that might want to kill Jon Garner.

During the investigation, Sandra's son, Wesley, came down to the sheriff's office to give a statement about his knowledge related to the case. Wes related to the police that he was very close to Jon and that he was very upset about the fact that his father had been killed. Wes told law enforcement that he did not believe his mother's story about an unknown intruder being the killer. Wes advised the police that his mother owned a .38-caliber handgun, the same type of weapon used to commit the murder. Wes also stated that his mother was in "bad health," suffering from multiple sclerosis. She had talked on more than one occasion about committing suicide.

The law enforcement authorities subsequently obtained a search warrant, authorized by a judge in Ellis County, to conduct a follow-up search of the Garner property. During the second search, the police confiscated all the electronics in the house, including Sandra's cellphone and iPad. An examination of the phone and iPad revealed some evidence that was essential to the case. The iPad disclosed that someone, using the device, had conducted a Google search on the issue of "16 Ways to Kill Someone and Get Away with It!" The police still lacked a "key piece of evidence," the murder weapon! Wesley was interviewed a second time about the location of the possible murder weapon. In the second interview, Wes disclosed that his mother sometimes hid money in her car. The police obtained an additional search warrant and searched Sandra's car that was parked in the garage. The search of her car resulted in the finding of a .38-caliber pistol that was wrapped in a wet towel. The gun was located under the front seat of the car. Sandra was brought to the Ellis County Sheriff's Office for another interview. Sandra denied any knowledge about the gun. Sandra was arrested and charged with murder.

The Court Proceedings

A felony charge of first-degree murder was filed against Sandra Garner in the district court of Ellis County, Texas, on January 10, 2018. During her arraignment a few days later, Sandra pleaded "*not guilty*" and requested a trial by jury. The court set her bond at $2 million. Sandra was unable to post the bond, and she remained in jail for the next eighteen months. Attorney Tom Pappas was selected to serve as her defense counsel in the case.

During the next several months, several motions were filed by the defense counsel to determine the strength of the state's case against Sandra Garner. Motions for discovery and inspection of all law enforcement records and reports were compiled during the police investigation. Some items were not available as ordered by the court. The missing items included pictures and videos recordings of the crime scene taken by law enforcement at the crime scene. Apparently, these items were lost or otherwise unavailable for review. Other questions were raised during the pretrial hearings, including the lack of testing evidence related to "gunpowder" residue on Sandra's hands on the night of the murder. The case was finally set for jury trial in the fall of 2019. The state prosecutors called more than 2S witnesses and introduced more than four hundred items into evidence to prove its case. The evidence included testimony by law enforcement officials from the Maypearl, Texas Police Department, the Ellis County Sheriff's Department, and state of Texas expert witnesses with regard to the autopsy results and the ballistics examination of the murder weapon. At the conclusion of the state's evidence, the prosecutors rested their case. The defense's motion to dismiss, based on insufficient evidence, was denied by the judge.

The Defense of Sandra Garner

The attorney for the defense, Tom Pappas, presented evidence in response to the state's case. Testimony presented included that Sandra Garner had met Jon Garner when they were employed by DHL Express. Jon was the district manager in charge of the local office. Sandra and Jon dated for several months and got married in 2000. Sandra was several years older than Jon and had two adult children from a prior marriage including a son named Wesley. Defense evidence supported the view that Jon Garner was killed by an unknown intruder who entered the Garner house at around 12:30 a.m. on January 2, 2018. Pappas presented evidence that Jon Garner was a difficult person to work for at the express company and that he had fired or terminated more than a dozen employees for various reasons in the last five years. Testimony indicated that

Jon was a heavy drinker who often bragged about his ownership of more than forty guns that were located throughout his house. Jon also bragged to family that he kept several thousand dollars around the house, money that he saved and stashed away in case that there was a national bank financial crisis.

Sandra Garner took the witness stand and testified that she and Jon were a close couple who had just celebrated their wedding anniversary a few days earlier. Sandra also stated that she had several medical issues and had been unable to work since 2012. Jon was her caretaker who had taken very good care of her the past several years. She had no reason whatsoever to want to kill Jon. With regard to the Google search, Sandra testified that Wesley was over at her house and on several occasions that he often used her iPad since he did not have a computer or access to the Internet. The defense then rested its case.

The Jury Verdict

The presiding judge then conducted a private meeting in the judge's chambers with the attorneys for the state and the defense present to review the jury instructions that the judge would give to the jury. Upon reconvening the trial in the courtroom, the judge delivered instructions to the jury on the rules of evidence and the legal requirements for the jury to deliver a proper verdict. The state's attorneys, bearing the burden of proof of "beyond a reasonable doubt," delivered their dosing arguments. The prosecutors argued that the credible evidence presented by law enforcement officers showed that the victim was killed by a .38-caliber pistol that was owned by the defendant and that the murder weapon had been found in Sandra Garner's car. The prosecutors also emphasized that the information retrieved from the defendant's iPad showed that she was looking for a way to kill her husband. The logical explanation was that Sandra Garner was the only person who had "the motive," "the means," and "the opportunity" to kill Jon Garner.

On the closing argument for the defense, her attorney, Tom Pappas, argued that Sandra Garner had "no reason or motive to kill" her husband. Jon was taking excellent care of her as her health issues got worse. Pappas emphasized that "a disgruntled ex-employee" from his place of employment would have the motive to kill Jon. The intruder wanted "revenge and the large sum of cash" that Jon kept inside the house. The defense counsel also argued that the defendant's son, Wesley Miller, had a motive to kill Jon Garner. Wesley needed money. A quick way to get it was kill Jon and take the $18,000 that was stashed inside the house. The defense argued that Wes was the most logical suspect.

After the closing arguments, the jury retired to deliberate and considered the conflicting evidence that had been presented during the monthlong trial. The jury deliberations started at approximately 5:00 p.m. on October 10, 2019. Three hours later, the jury foreman notified the court bailiff that they had reached a verdict. A few minutes later, the judge reconvened the court and asked the bailiff to bring the jury in from the jury room. The judge inquired as whether the jury had reached a verdict. The foreman advised the judge that "we have reached a verdict." The bailiff took possession of the paperwork and turned it over to the judge. The judge reviewed the "verdict forms" and indicated that they were in the proper form. The judge then read into the record: "State of Texas v. Sandra Garner, we, the jury, find the defendant, Sandra Garner, *not guilty.*" The people in the courtroom were totally shocked. The judge thanked the jury for their service and excused them from further jury service. The judge ordered the clerk to record the verdict and ordered that the defendant, Sandra Garner, be released from the Ellis County Jail immediately. Sandra was returned to the Ellis County Jail for the filing of the proper paperwork. Sandra was released from custody approximately an hour later. Sandra Garner was a free woman at last. Sandra had spent the past eighteen months in jail for a crime that an Ellis County jury said that she did not commit, the murder of Jon Garner. Sandra continues to live in the same house today. Sandra has the love and support of her daughter. However, Sandra is estranged from her son, Wesley Miller. Sandra has not spoken to Wesley in several years.

Who Killed Jon Garner?

The unresolved question is who killed Jon Garner on January 2, 2018. The possible suspects are the following:

1. Sandra Garner? An Ellis County jury composed of twelve citizens of the community concluded that she was not guilty of the murder on October 10, 2019. Could the jury be wrong? Did Sandra Garner get away with murder?
2. Wesley Miller, the estranged son of Sandra Garner? The evidence presented during the trial of the case indicated that Wes had the means, the opportunity, and a possible motive for the murder. Wes needed money. Jon had several thousand dollars stashed in the house. Wes had access to the house, use of the electronics in the house and access the murder weapon. Additionally, Wes gave a statement to law enforcement indicating that his own natural mother, Sandra, was the person who may have killed Jon. Why would Wesley do that? Possibly, he wanted to divert the attention of law enforcement away from himself as a possible suspect.
3. An unidentified person was the intruder. Sandra described the intruder as a disgruntled ex-employee who had been fired by Jon Garner several months earlier while working for DHL Express. The intruder somehow had knowledge about a large sum of money that Jon kept stashed in the house. The intruder also knew about the large stash of guns that Jon had hidden throughout the house.
4. An unidentified person who knew about the stash of guns and cash that Jon Garner kept in the house. Jon had a reputation of being a "heavy drinker" who bragged about his "money and guns."

Who killed Jon Garner on January 2, 2018? This is an "unsolved mystery"!

THE COP KILLER
New York v. Barbara Sheehan (2008)

Barbara Sheehan was born Barbara Henry in Howard County, New York, in 1961. While attending high school, Barbara met Raymond Sheehan at a church social event at the Lady of Grace Church, where Raymond's brother was the minister.

The pair immediately "hit it off" and started dating on a regular basis. Three years later, Raymond got a job with the New York City Police Department. Eventually, Raymond proposed that they get married and move to New York City. Barbara accepted the proposal, and the couple were married in 1984. Two years later, the couple was graced with the birth of a beautiful daughter whom they named Jennifer Joyce. Approximately two years later, a beautiful young boy was born to the couple. They chose to name him Raymond Sheehan Jr. While Raymond worked the midnight shift, serving as a patrolman for the police department, Barbara cared for the children. During the day, Barbara worked for the New York City public school system while Raymond cared for the children. During the day, Raymond would often call Barbara at work, complaining that he needed help with the kids. Barbara would be forced to leave her workplace and rush home to help him. Arriving home, Barbara would take care of the needs of the kids while Raymond would consume several cans of beer. Raymond would "fly into a rage" about the kids' behavior and verbally insult Barbara, stating that the kids were "little brats" and that Barbara was a lousy mother.

Later, Raymond's anger would accelerate to acts of physical violence. Raymond would push and shove Barbara, telling her that she was "fat," "stupid," and a "lousy housekeeper." Occasionally, he would punch her in the back, arms, and chest. In 1994, Raymond attended a "bachelor party" at his brother's house. Raymond came home drunk and started beating Barbara, striking her in the face and head. One punch was so severe that Barbara sustained an injury to her left ear, breaking her left eardrum. The next morning, Barbara walked into the bathroom to take a shower. Looking in the mirror, Barbara noticed that she had two "black eyes" sustained from Raymond's assault the night before. On every occasion, Raymond would "sober up" and apologize for his behavior and promise "to never beat her up" again. The physical abuse of Barbara accelerated when Raymond was promoted to the rank of sergeant and placed in charge of the "homicide division" in his precinct within the police department. Raymond would bring home "pictures of dead bodies" taken at a crime scene and show them to Barbara. Raymond would threaten her with statements like "this is what is going to happen to you if you ever try to leave me!" Barbara would assure him that she loved him and that she would never do that to him.

In 2005, the Sheehan family went to Lake Geneva for a vacation. Raymond got drunk and started beating on Barbara again. She sustained a black eye and bruises over her chest and stomach. In addition to his abusive behavior, Raymond was paranoid that someone was "trying to kill him." Raymond would carry two guns with him at all times. Raymond told Barbara that he was going to shoot her if she ever attempted to take the kids and leave him.

In 2007, Barbara and Raymond took a vacation to the Caribbean, traveling to a posh resort in Jamaica. Barbara woke Raymond up from an afternoon nap so that they could go down to party on the beach. Raymond flew into a rage and started beating Barbara. Raymond grabbed her by the hair of her head and started slamming her head against a concrete wall. Barbara's injuries were so severe that she had to seek medical attention. Raymond rushed Barbara downstairs and took a cab to a nearby hospital. Barbara's injuries required over a dozen stitches to her head in order to close the wound. On the plane ride home, Raymond promised to stop drinking and start attending AA meetings. Barbara also suggested that they attend marital counseling sessions to resolve the problems in their marriage. Raymond readily agreed.

Despite all the promises of reform from Raymond, things remained the same. Raymond continued to drink heavily, often consuming a twelve-pack of beer when he got off his shift at the police department. Raymond refused to attend the local AA meetings and would not attend marital counseling appointments that Barbara had set up. Barbara would have to attend the sessions by herself or cancel the sessions altogether. Raymond retired from the New York City Police Department in 2005 after twenty years of service. The drinking accelerated. Raymond started drinking hard liquor, and the spousal abuse occurred on a daily basis. Jennifer got a job and moved into her own apartment. Raymond Jr. enrolled in a college in Connecticut and left. With both kids gone, Raymond's abuse reached a breaking point!

The Murder of Raymond Sheehan

In January 2008, Raymond wanted to go on vacation to a beach resort in Florida. Reflecting on the terrible experience that had occurred in Jamaica, Barbara refused. Raymond had already made reservations to go. Barbara was adamant: "No way!"

On February 17, 2008, Raymond and Barbara drove up to Connecticut to visit with Raymond Jr. On the way back to the city, Raymond started arguing again about the Florida vacation. The anger accelerated into a physical brawl. Raymond started hitting her in the face. Barbara tried to get out of the car. Raymond struck her in the head, breaking her nose. Raymond stopped by the local hospital emergency room to have Barbara treated by an ER doctor. Hospital personnel inquired about how the injuries occurred. Barbara lied and told them that she had fallen in the bathtub, striking her face on the side of the bathtub. Barbara was given first aid and released to go home.

Early on the morning of February 18, 2008, Raymond dragged Barbara out of bed and demanded that she call the travel agent and change the schedule on the vacation so that they could leave immediately. During the argument, Raymond pulled out his Glock pistol and threatened to shoot. Barbara relented and agreed to go. Raymond went into the bathroom to take a shower while Barbara was on the phone with the travel agent. While Raymond was in the shower, Barbara remembered that Raymond kept a second gun in the closet. Barbara retrieved the gun and walked into the bathroom. Barbara raised the gun and shot Raymond as he was getting out of the shower.

Despite sustaining wounds to several parts of his body, Raymond struggled to get to his Glock pistol that was lying on the bathroom sink. Barbara grabbed the Glock pistol away from Raymond and fired six more shots into Raymond from close range. Raymond fell to the floor of the bathroom and passed out. Barbara kneeled down beside of him on the bathroom floor and uttered, "You will never hurt me again, you bastard."

Backing away, Barbara sat down on the stool and waited for Raymond to die. Barbara waited almost an hour before calling 911 to summon an ambulance and the police. In approximately twenty minutes, two police officers arrived and assisted the medics into loading Raymond into an ambulance to be transported to the local hospital.

Upon arriving at the Sheehan residence, the police recognized the victim as a retired New York City police officer, Raymond Sheehan. After securing the crime scene and assessing the situation, the police placed Barbara under arrest and advised her of her Miranda rights. Barbara, waiving her right to remain silent, stated that she shot Raymond after he threatened to kill her earlier that morning. Barbara was placed in handcuffs and transported to the police station for formal booking. The charge to be filed: "murder one." Additional charges of assault with a deadly weapon and illegal possession of a firearm were added later. Upon being arraigned on the charges in the Supreme Court of New York, Barbara entered a plea of "*not guilty*" and requested a jury trial. Due to the large backlog of criminal cases pending in the supreme courts of New York City, the case could not be set for trial until three years later.

The Trial of Barbara Sheehan

The jury trial for Barbara Sheehan started in September 2011 in New York Supreme Court with Judge Barry Kron presiding over the trial. During the first phase of the trial, prospective jurors were called before the court to answer questions about the case and their ability to give both the state of New York and Barbara Sheehan a fair trial. Ultimately, a jury panel composed of nine women and three men was sworn in to serve on the Sheehan trial. The evidence presented by the state was quite simple!

Barbara Sheehan had shot Raymond Sheehan with two different guns on the morning of February 18, 2008, in the bathroom of their residence. Barbara had confessed to the killing of Raymond. The medical examiner testified that the cause of death was multiple gunshot wounds to the torso and head of Raymond. A total of eleven bullets were extracted from the remains of the victim. According to law enforcement, the case was clearly first-degree murder and the defendant should be given a sentence of "life in prison." The prosecutor rested his case, and the burden shifted to the defense counsel to present evidence showing the facts and circumstances behind the homicide. Barbara was represented by a widely respected criminal defense attorney, Michael Dowd. Barbara was the key witness to testify in her own defense. After taking the stand, Barbara related the history of her marriage to Raymond. Barbara stated that for the first few years of their marriage, she and Raymond were happy newlyweds.

The marriage changed dramatically after the birth of their children, Jennifer and Ray Jr. Raymond would come home from work and start drinking beer. On a typical evening, he would consume a twelve-pack of beer. Being drunk, Raymond would get angry with her and the kids. Barbara related that over the years, Raymond would become physically violent, punching and kicking her in front of the kids. The violence escalated after Raymond was promoted to the rank of sergeant and assigned to head "the violent crimes" unit of the New York City Police Department. Raymond would get more violent every year. Barbara related the occasions when he assaulted her while they were on vacation and the numerous trips to the hospital for treatment of the injuries received during these beatings. After three days of grueling testimony and cross-examination by the state's attorney, Barbara was excused from the witness stand. Jennifer, her daughter, then took the stand and related the many instances when she observed her father assaulting and beating her mother. Jennifer related that Raymond had several guns in the house and he would threaten to use them on her mother, her brother, and herself. Ray Jr. testified to the fact that his father would punch, kick, and beat his mother at least once a week. Ray related that he had emotional problems resulting from his parents constant fighting. Ray stated that he thought about committing "suicide" to get away from the daily nightmare. Ray's home life was the principal reason he chose to go to college in Connecticut.

During the final days of the trial, the defense counsel, Michael Dowd, called an "expert witness," Dr. Jacqueline Campbell, to the witness stand. Dr. Campbell was a professor of psychology at Johns Hopkins University in New York. Dr. Campbell was considered an expert in the field of psychiatry dealing with the issue of the battered women's syndrome. Dr. Campbell testified a woman in marital environment where there was physical violence experiences a state of "being trapped and totally helpless." Evidence of escalating violence, the presence of guns, and threats to kill would make any woman feel totally helpless. Judge Kron limited Dr. Campbell's testimony to limited general information about the issue of being "a battered woman." Dr. Campbell was not allowed to give her expert opinion that Barbara Sheehan was the classical example of being "a battered woman." At the conclusion of the evidence, the judge gave the jury instructions on how to weigh the evidence and render a proper verdict. After closing arguments, the jury retired and began their deliberations. Tensions mounted on both sides as the jury continued their deliberations for three days. That length of time was considered an extremely long time for a jury to render a verdict. The parties on both sides were concerned that the jury was deadlocked and that the judge would have to declare a mistrial and excuse the jury. Finally, on October 6, 2011, the jury returned with its verdict. The unanimous decision of the jury: the defendant, Barbara Sheehan, was *not guilty* of the crime of murder. Everyone in the courtroom was shocked by the verdict! The jury did find Barbara guilty of the lesser crime of criminal possession of a firearm. Judge Kron set judgment and sentencing for Barbara Sheehan on November 10, 2011.

On November 10, 2011, the Supreme Court of the state of New York in the case of Barbara Sheehan convened. Judge Roy Kron, the trial judge, had the final authority to determine the final punishment that should be imposed on Barbara for the verdict of the jury on the charge of criminal possession of a firearm. After hearing arguments of counsel, Judge Kron ordered Barbara to serve the maximum punishment of "*five years in prison.*" The defense counsel advised the court that the defendant would appeal the conviction and the sentence. The trial judge set bond at $1 million for Barbara to remain out of jail while awaiting the appeal. With the help of family and her supporters, Barbara was able to post the million-dollar bail and be released from custody pending the outcome of the appeal.

The Appellate Decision

On her appeal to the New York Supreme Court, Barbara contended that there were two principal issues in the trial that constituted reversible error. These issues were the following:

1. Judge Kron committed reversible error by refusing to allow the entire testimony of Dr. Jacqueline Campbell. The jury was not allowed to hear the assessment of Dr. Campbell that the facts of the Barbara Sheehan case was a classic example of the "battered women's syndrome!"
2. The sentence and punishment of five years in prison was excessive.

The appeal was denied on May 29, 2013, and Barbara was forced to serve the four-year sentence. Barbara was released from prison in 2016, and she is enjoying her grandkids, living in New York.

Analysis of the Barbara Sheehan Case

The Sheehan case is a very controversial case in American legal history with regard to the recognition of the concept of the "battered women's syndrome." Does a woman in a violent marital relationship have the right to use deadly force against her husband? During the Sheehan trial, the defense presented "expert witness" testimony from a renowned psychologist, Dr. Jacqueline Campbell, relative to the mental state of a woman who is trapped in a marital relationship with an abusive husband. However, the trial judge refused to allow the jury to hear evidence that Barbara Sheehan was a clear example of being "a battered woman." Despite this testimony, the jury decided that Barbara was not guilty to the charge of first-degree murder. The jury only convicted Barbara of a lesser crime: criminal possession of a firearm. Why would a jury find Sheehan "not guilty" on the charge of murder? Sheehan readily admitted that she shot her husband, Raymond, eleven times using two different guns on the morning of February 18, 2008? Why?

1. The jury was composed of nine women and only three men. The women on the jury may have had a great deal of compassion for the woman who was trapped in an abusive marriage with a retired police officer.
2. The jury may have been persuaded by the limited testimony that Dr. Campbell did present to the typical characteristics of a woman being the victim of an abusive husband. The jury appeared to render the proper verdict considering all the factors that may have forced Barbara Sheehan to end her "abusive marriage" by killing her husband.

A DEADLY CRASH
Connecticut v. Cherelle Baldwin (2013)

Cherelle Baldwin graduated from high school in Bridgeport Connecticut in 2010. With her friendly smile and warm personality. Cherelle was able to get a great job with a local medical center within a few weeks after her graduation. With a good job, Cherelle went out and purchased a nice used car and secured her own rental house. During a social outing with friends one weekend, Cherelle was introduced to Jeffrey Brown. Cherelle was impressed with his demeanor and friendly personality. They exchanged phone numbers. Jeffrey promised to call her in a few days. True to his word, Jeffrey called Cherelle and asked her to go out to dinner with him the following weekend. Cherelle accepted his invitation and accompanied him to an elegant seafood restaurant. The date was outstanding! Cherelle and Jeffrey starting dating, going out to the movies and other social events in the Bridgeport area. Within a few weeks, the couple became inseparable, spending the weekends together. Approximately six months into their relationship, Cherelle found out that she was pregnant with Jeffrey's child. Cherelle gave birth to a boy in the fall of 2011. Jeffrey adored the young boy they named Jeffrey Brown Junior! Cherelle allowed her mother to take care of her child so that she could return to work at the medical center. Jeffrey adopted his young son, and the relationship appeared to going well until Cherelle discovered Jeffrey's true occupation: he was a drug dealer and major distributor of illegal drugs in the Bridgeport area. Cherelle confronted Jeffrey one weekend about the evidence that she had uncovered. Jeffrey denied the allegations and became very hostile toward Cherelle, telling her to ignore the "hearsay crap" that she had heard from some old woman at the medical facility where she worked. Cherelle cried and accepted his explanation. She apologized for making false accusation.

The Day of the Murder (May 18, 2013)

Despite Jeffrey's denial that he was involved in drug trafficking, Cherelle noticed many instances of "odd behavior" by Jeffrey in 2012. These included frequent trips out of town, strange phone calls at all hours of the day, and Jeffrey always carrying a gun around with him. What was Jeffrey doing? Cherelle concluded that Jeffrey was engaged in some sort of criminal activity. If that was the case, Cherelle concluded that she and her young son could be in danger. Reaching the breaking point, one Sunday afternoon, Cherelle told Jeffrey that their relationship was over. Jeffrey became very upset, yelling and screaming at Cherelle. Jeffrey assaulted and punched Cherelle, knocking her to the floor. A few days later, Jeffrey returned to Cherelle's house, trying to reconcile with her. Cherelle refused to allow him into the house. Jeffrey pushed his way in and started beating her up. A neighbor called the police who arrived within ten minutes. Jeffrey was arrested and taken to jail after Cherelle signed a "domestic assault" offense report against him. Cherelle got a "protective order" issued by a judge of the Connecticut court system, prohibiting Jeffrey from coming over to her house or having any communications with her. Despite the court order, Jeffrey continued to harass and threaten Cherelle with phone calls and text messages. During the twenty-four period prior to the homicide, Jeffrey sent Cherelle twelve text messages, telling her that he was coming over to her house and that he was going kill her that night. In the early morning hours of May 18, 2013, Cherelle was awakened by the sound of Jeffrey breaking into her house. Jeffrey beat her, strangled her, and whipped her with a belt.

Cherelle ran outside and jumped into her car, trying to get away. Jeffrey followed her. Starting her car, Cherelle slammed the car into gear as Jeffrey ran in front of the car. Hitting the gas pedal, Cherelle rammed the car into Jeffrey as he ran in front of her. The car lurched forward, slamming Jeffrey into a concrete wall near the driveway. Cherelle slowly backed the car up and shut off the motor. Cherelle observed that Jeffrey was lying in the driveway, dead from being crushed by her car!

The Police Investigation

Hearing the crash outside, a neighbor called 911 for the Bridgeport Police Department. Officers arrived at the scene within approximately fifteen minutes. Cherelle was still inside her car, totally stunned by the accident. Police officers, after examining the body lying in the driveway, summoned for paramedics and an ambulance. An officer approached Cherelle, asking her what happened. Cherelle told the officer that she did not know what had happened! Cherelle felt severe pain and discomfort in her left leg. She could not get out of her car. The officer advised her to relax! An ambulance was on the way. Cherelle was taken to a local hospital where the emergency room doctor determined that she had a broken leg. A cast was applied to her leg. After her injuries were treated at the hospital, police officers questioned Cherelle about what had happened. Cherelle advised the officers that the man had broken into her house and assaulted her. Trying to get away, she fled out the front door and jumped into her car. Cherelle stated that she did not remember exactly what happened after that, that she passed out and was unconscious for several minutes. Concluding their interrogation, the police allowed Cherelle to leave the hospital and go home.

Cherelle went to stay with her mother for a few days as she recovered from her leg injury. Detectives with the Bridgeport Police Department contacted her a few days later and asked her to come down to the police station for a follow-up interview. With the assistance of her mother, Cherelle proceeded down to the police station. Because of her severe leg injury, Cherelle entered the building at the police station in a wheelchair. Cherelle was escorted to an "interview room" and interrogated by two detectives with the Bridgeport Police Department. Cherelle answered all their questions. After two hours, Cherelle was allowed to leave. The detectives told her that they would contact her later!

Murder Charges Filed against Cherelle Baldwin

On June 5, 2013, Cherelle Baldwin was arrested and taken the Bridgeport Municipal Jail. Two days later, Cherelle appeared in a Connecticut courtroom and was formally charged with first-degree murder. Cherelle entered a plea of "not guilty" and demanded a trial by jury. Local criminal defense attorney Miles Gerety was selected to represent Cherelle. In July 2013, Cherelle Baldwin was bound over for trial on the charge of murder one. The trial court set bail at $1 million. Cherelle was unable to post bail and was remanded to custody of the Connecticut Department of Corrections. The case was delayed in the Connecticut court system and did not come up for trial until January 2015. During the trial, the state attorney general's office portrayed Cherelle as "a cold-blooded murderer" who enticed Jeffrey Brown over to her house on the morning of May 18, 2013, with the intent to kill him and tell the police that he was a "burglar" that she killed when he broke into her house. The defense presented evidence, including Cherelle's own testimony, that Jeffrey Brown was an ex-boyfriend who had previously been convicted of assaulting her and was under a "restraining order" which prohibited him from coming around Cherelle and her son. The jury retired and deliberated for more than twelve hours over a two-day period before returning to court, advising the judge that the jury was unable to reach a verdict. The judge declared a mistrial and ordered the case reset for trial at a later day. A polling of the jury, after the mistrial, indicated that the jury was deadlocked with eleven jurors voting to find Cherelle "not guilty" of the crime of murder. One juror held out, saying Cherelle was guilty!

The Second Trial of Cherelle Baldwin

Despite a verdict of eleven to one for acquittal in the first trial, the state's attorney demanded that Cherelle Baldwin be tried again on the charge of murder. The second trial was delayed for over one year due to the crowded Connecticut court system. Cherelle remained in the custody of the Connecticut Department of Corrections during the delay. The case was finally set for trial in March 2016. The same evidence was presented to the second jury. The result: a jury panel of seven women and five men found Cherelle Baldwin "*not guilty*" of the crime of *murder one*! Cherelle collapsed on the floor of the courtroom when she heard the verdict. The trial judge accepted the verdict and ordered that charges be dismissed and that Cherelle be released from custody immediately! Cherelle walked out a Connecticut courtroom on March 31, 2016, free at last, after almost three years behind bars! Cherelle has slowly tried to put her life back together! Cherelle was arrested when she was twenty-one years of age. Her son, Jeffrey, was only one year old when she was arrested and placed in jail. Jeffrey was now four years old. Cherelle had missed so much of her life while she was in prison. It was extremely difficult for Cherelle to regain those three lost years that she had spent in prison. Cherelle has been diagnosed by mental health professionals as suffering from "post-traumatic stress" syndrome. Cherelle still has nightmares today as a result of the homicide and the years that she spent in prison.

Analysis of the Cherelle Baldwin Case

The Cherelle Baldwin case is a sad chapter in the American Criminal Justice System. A man broke into a woman's home and assaulted her in the middle of the night. The man was an "ex-boyfriend" against whom she had a "restraining order" issued by a Connecticut court prohibiting him from having any contact with her. Fleeing the house after the assault, Cherelle ran over the man with her car in her own driveway! How could the police and the prosecutor pursue charges against Cherelle under those circumstances? Did Cherelle have the "right of self-defense" when confronted by an intruder that assaulted her inside her own house? There are several factors to consider in analyzing the Cherelle Baldwin case. These include the following:

1. Cherelle Baldwin is an "Afro-American woman." Did race place a factor in the prosecution's decision to pursue first-degree murder charges against her? Would a White

woman be prosecuted under these circumstances? Highly unlikely!

2. The first trial of Cherelle Baldwin ended in a mistrial after the jury was unable to reach a verdict. However, the vote was eleven to one in favor of finding Cherelle innocent of the crime. Why would the prosecutor demand a second trial when 90 percent of the jury in the first trial concluded that she was not guilty? Was race a factor in the decision in the state's decision to demand a second trial?

3. The most significant factor to consider in the Cherelle Baldwin case is the extraordinary outrageous bond that was set in her case, to wit, $1 million. Cherelle was unable to post that high bond and was forced to remain in jail for nearly three years until she got her day in court. That is outrageous! After the mistrial in the first case, the bond should have been reduced for to a lower amount, thereby allowing Cherelle to be released from jail pending the second trial.

The entire trial process in the Cherelle Baldwin case was "a miscarriage of justice" that should never be allowed to occur in the American criminal justice system ever again!

THE DEAD BOYFRIEND
Florida v. Stacy Sabo (2018)

Stacy Sabo was born and raised in the "sunshine state" of Florida. Stacy loved the warm summer climate and enjoyed spending time at the beach with her friends.

Having endured one foiled marriage, Stacy was reluctant to consider serious dating for a few years. Her lady friends had introduced Stacy to several young men over the years since her divorce. Most of the men on these dates were younger men, looking for a "one-night stand." That was not the type of relationship that Stacy wanted. Stacy wanted a long-term relationship with a "mature man" who was interested in more than just "sex"! One evening, Stacy went out with some of her girlfriends to local nightclub to relax and enjoy the music. During the evening, Stacy was introduced a man named Brock Dion. Brock had a friendly smile and a warm personality. Stacy was impressed with his ability to tell humorous stories about his life experiences.

At the end of the evening, Brock requested her phone number, telling her that he would like to take her out to dinner one evening. Stacy eagerly agreed and gave Brock her phone number. A few days later, Brock called Stacy and invited her out to dinner the following weekend, Stacy and Brock had a nice dinner at a seafood restaurant near the beach. Stacy and Brock started dating, going out every weekend. Brock took Stacy to meet his mother who lived in Leisure Village, Florida. The ladies "hit it off" immediately. Stacy started thinking that she had finally found her man. The future seemed so exciting! Little did Stacy know, within a few months, Brock would be the victim of a homicide in the front yard at his mother's house. Who killed Brock Dion? It was Stacy!

The Day of the Murder (November 24, 2018)

Stacy worked for a large Fortune 500 company based in Florida. During a relaxing day at home one weekend, Stacy decided to do a "Google search" on her laptop, looking up information on various vacations involving a "cruise in the Caribbean." Stacy was dreaming about a romantic cruise with Brock in the near future. An ideal spot to discuss their future and the possibility of marriage. Stacy was searching through one website when she decided to do a random search on Brock. Checking through a public records database for the state of Florida, Stacy ran a "records check" on Brock. After a few minutes search, Stacy was shocked to see that Brock had a prior criminal record resulting from several "drunk driving" arrests. Was Brock was "an alcoholic"? Brock had never shown any signs of being a "problem drinker." While Brock had experienced some recent issues related to losing his job, he seemed to have adjusted to the situation. Brock was living with his mother until he got back on his feet. Stacy was about to end her search when she saw that Brock's driver's license had been revoked by the Florida Department of Public Safety.

Stacy panicked! Brock was driving her car! What would happen if he was caught driving "drunk" in her car? What if he had an accident while driving her car? Would she be sued in a lawsuit for allowing a "drunk" to drive her car? Stacy left her residence and headed over to Leisure Village to talk to Brock about what she had found out. Stacy phoned Brock and told him that she wanted to talk to him and to meet her outside in the yard of his mother's house. Stacy did not want Brock's mother to hear the conversation about his DUI driving record.

Arriving at the residence in Leisure Village, Stacy pulled up in the driveway and saw Brock coming out the front door of his mother's house. Stacy stepped out of the car and started to ask Brock about his driving her car with a suspended driver's license. Stacy demanded that Brock hand over the keys to her car. Stacy told Brock that she did not want him driving her car anymore if he did not have a valid driver's license. Brock became incensed at Stacy's hostile attitude toward him. Brock started cursing Stacy and picked up a large pail located on the front porch. Lounging forward, Brock threw the bucket at her. Stacy dodged the pail and begged Brock to stop and listen to her questions. She wanted answers to her questions about his drunk driving arrests and why Brock's driver's license had been suspended by the Florida Department of Public Safety. Brock reached down and picked up a concrete yard ornament and threw it toward Stacy's head. Stacy jumped back and told Brock to stop.

Brock ignored her requests and starting moving toward her, telling her that he was going "to shut her up." Stacy moved backward and reached into her handbag. Stacy pulled out her gun, "a 9 mm revolver" and pointed it at Brock. Stacy told Brock to stop or that she was going to shoot. Brock continued moving toward Stacy. Backing up, Stacy fired her weapon at Brock. *Bam!* The bullet from Stacy's pistol struck Brock in the chest. Brock fell to the ground. Stacy was in a state of shock! Placing her gun back in her handbag, Stacy paused for a second and then rushed up to Brock. Stacy attempted to perform CPR on Brock. The effort was not successful. Grabbing her cellphone from her purse, Stacy called 911 for the Martin County Sheriff's Office to summon an ambulance. Brock was transported to the local hospital. Brock died in the emergency room. Stacy was taken to the sheriff's office to give a formal statement to law enforcement about the events that led up to the shooting.

The Law Enforcement Investigation

Stacy Sabo was subjected to a lengthy interrogation at the Martin County, Florida, sheriff's office on November 25, 2018. During the interview, Stacy gave a detailed statement about the events that led up to the shooting of Brock Dion that afternoon. When questioned about the weapon that had used in the shooting, Stacy advised the sheriff that she had a "conceal-carry permit" issued by the state of Florida and that she was legally authorized to carry the weapon under Florida law. The sheriff's office also interviewed several individuals who lived in Leisure Village where the incident occurred. The accounts of the witnesses verified the events that occurred prior to the time of the shooting. Stacy was released from custody and advised that the sheriff's office would finish their investigation and consult with the Florida Attorney General's Office about the results of their investigation. The sheriff's office verified that Stacy Sabo did have a license to carry the weapon. Stacy's permit was issued after she had completed the required firearms training mandated under Florida law. As a part of their investigation, the sheriff's office conducted a background check into the criminal history of Brock Dion with regard to law enforcement. The completed records check disclosed that Brock Dion had an extensive criminal history going back more than twenty years. Brock's prior record indicated that he had been arrested for drunk driving on several occasions. Additionally, Brock had been arrested for domestic violence, possession of drugs, assault and battery, resisting arrest, and eluding law enforcement. A few days, the sheriff issued a public statement indicating that no criminal charges would be filed against Stacy Sabo relating to the shooting.

Analysis of the Stacy Sabo Case

The decision of law enforcement to not seek criminal charges against Stacy Sabo was based on several factors. These factors include the following:

1. When may a person use "deadly force"? The standard law in many jurisdictions is the Stand Your Ground principle:

    A person may use deadly force if he or she is legally on the property for a legitimate purpose. In this case, Stacy was legally on the property for the purpose of retrieving her car keys from her boyfriend, Brock Dion. Stacy's concern was that she did not want Brock driving her car if his driver's license had been revoked by the Florida Department of Public Safety.

2. The Stand Your Ground principle further indicates that if the person is placed in "imminent danger" of serious bodily

harm by the victim, that person may use their weapon for their own personal safety. In this case, Stacy was the victim of an aggressive assault by Brock Dion: he threw two different objects at her, trying to injure or kill her.

3. The third factor was the prior criminal record of Brock Dion. The records check by the Martin County Sheriff's Office indicated that Brock Dion had more than twenty arrests in the past fifteen years and that he had a history of domestic violence with regard to women.

All of these factors resulted in a mandate from the Florida Attorney General's Office that no charges should be filed against Stacy Sabo in the death of Brock Dion.

THE MURDER OF
MATT WINKLER
Tennessee v. Mary Winkler

On a cool December morning, December 10, 1973, Mary Carol
Freeman was born in Knoxville, Tennessee. Mary was the beautiful
daughter of proud parents, Clark and Mary Freeman. Clark Freeman
was a very successful real estate broker in Knoxville. Mary was an ele-
mentary school teacher. Mary was raised in a Christian environment.
The entire family attended weekly services at the Laurel Church of
Christ in Knoxville. Mary went through the Knoxville public school
system by the name of Carol Freeman. Mary Carol was very active
in high school, belonging to Spanish club, the high school choir, and
the Future Teachers of America club. Carol graduated from South
Doyle High School in 1992. Aspiring to follow in her mother's footsteps, Carol enrolled in college, Freedman-Hardeman University in
Henderson, Tennessee.

Matthew Winkler, the son of Dan and Diane Winkler, was a
very active high school student, playing both football and basketball.
Matt graduated from Austin High School in Decatur, Alabama in
1993. Matt decided to follow in his father's footsteps and become
a Church of Christ minister. Matt enrolled at Freed-Hardeman
University with a major in Ministerial Studies. Matt met Mary at a
social function at the university. Less than two years later, 1997, they
decided to get married in Nashville, Tennessee. A few months later,
Mary Carol gave birth to their first child, Patricia Ann. In 2000,
Mary gave birth to a second child, Allie. In 2005, Mary gave birth
to a third child, Brenna. The Winklers moved to Selmer, Tennessee,

in early 2005 when Matt obtained a position as the minister at the Fourth Street Church of Christ. The Winkler family seemed, for all intents and purposes, to be the ideal Christian family, with three adorable children. Appearances can be deceiving! Less than fifteen months later, Matt Winkler was found dead in the family home, killed by a shotgun blast in the back!

On the early morning hours of March 22, 2006, Mary Winkler was awakened by the alarm clock that went off at 6:15 a.m. Mary turned the alarm off and slowly got out of the large bed she shared with her husband, Matthew. Mary glanced over at her husband who was sound asleep, lying on his left side, facing away from Mary. Moving very quietly, Mary walked out of the bedroom and crept over to a closet. Quietly opening the closet door, Mary carefully removed a loaded twelve-gauge shotgun from the closet. Mary checked the gun to make sure that it was loaded. It was fully loaded. Mary crept slowly back into the bedroom and approached her side of the bed. Mary raised the shotgun up, pointing it toward her husband's back. Mary paused for a moment. Suddenly, the gun exploded—*boom!*— striking Matthew directly in the back. The impact of the blast knocked Matthew out of the bed and onto the floor. The shotgun blast put seventy-seven pellets of birdshot into Matthew Winkler's body, breaking his spine and destroying several organs. Mary walked over to check on Matthew. He was still breathing. Matthew uttered one final word: "Why?" Mary told him, "I am sorry!" Mary said she had to do that! "She could not take his abuse anymore." Mary took the gun outside and put it in the family SUV. Walking back into the house, Mary woke up her daughters and told them to get dressed. She explained that they had to leave the house immediately! Mary loaded the girls into the family SUV and left town within thirty minutes. Mary drove south, heading to Alabama. The next day, members of Church of Christ came to check on their minister when he did not show up for church services. Church members found the parsonage locked up. Retrieving a key from the church, the members found Matt Winkler dead inside the house. A 911 call to the local police department got an officer on the crime scene within twenty minutes. Upon entering the house, the police determined that the minister had been the "victim of a murder" and the pastor's wife and children were missing!

The Police Investigation

Law enforcement personnel arrived at the Winkler household on the evening of March 23, 2006, at approximately 9:30 p.m. The initial investigation revealed that Matt Winkler had been dead for more than twelve hours. His body was removed from the crime scene and transported to the to the coroner's office for an autopsy examination. Law enforcement officials ascertained that the family vehicle was missing along his wife, Mary Winkler, and the three children. Tennessee authorities issued an "AMBER alert" for the family and the missing SUV, a Toyota minivan. Within forty-eight hours, the family vehicle was located in Orange Beach, Alabama. The vehicle was stopped by the Orange Beach police for a minor traffic violation. After checking out the van, Mary was arrested by Alabama authorities and taken to the local police station. Tennessee authorities were notified immediately and requested that Mary be held for questioning.

Mary agreed to answer questions by the local police. Mary's only concern was the welfare of her children. The children were taken into "protective custody" and later returned their grandparents, Dan and Diane Winkler. During the initial interrogation at the Orange Beach police department, Mary freely admitted that she and Matthew had "a heated argument" on the evening of March 21, 2006. The couple argued about "money issues" and the fact that their bank account was "overdrawn" by several thousand dollars. Matthew became very upset, telling Mary that their money problems were all due to her overspending and mismanagement of their bank account. Matt threatened her with physical violence several times that evening. The next morning, Mary admitted that she awoke at around 6:15, went to the closet, retrieved Matt's shotgun, and shot him in the back while he was sleeping!

Extradition proceedings were commenced by Tennessee authorities, and Mary Winkler was returned to Tennessee within a few weeks. A special grand jury heard the state's evidence in the case, returning an "indictment" charging Mary Winkler with first-degree murder on June 12, 2006. Mary Winkler was arraigned on June 30 and entered a plea of "*not guilty*"! Winkler's bond was set at $750,000! Since Mary was unable to post the bond, she was remanded to the McNairy County Jail. Mary's father eventually posted her bond, and she was released from jail about ninety days later. Attorneys Steve Farese and Leslie Ballin were selected to serve as her defense counsel. On the advice of counsel, Mary Winkler waived her right to a preliminary hearing. The case was set for a jury trial in McNairy County in the spring 2007. During the months leading up to the trial, Mary was directed by her attorneys to undergo psychological counseling for her mental health issues. Dr. Lynne Zager was assigned to treat and counsel Mary Winkler during the months leading up to the trial. During this period, the defense team started using the print and electronic media to draw attention to the issue of the plight of Mary Winkler and the alleged abuse that she suffered from Matt during their nearly ten years of marriage.

An article appeared in *Glamour* magazine featuring an interview with Mary's father, Clark Freeman. Mr. Freeman stated that Mary was the subject of mental and physical abuse by Matthew for most of their marriage. People supporting Mary appeared on *Good Morning, America* and also indicated that Mary Winkler had be "the victim" of mental and physical abuse by Matthew during the last five years of their troubled marriage. The pretrial publicity by the defense team revealed the defense strategy for the upcoming trial. Mary would be portrayed as "an abused wife" who had been forced to kill her husband!

The Winkler Trial

In the months leading up to the trial, there were several discussions about a possible plea bargain in the case. The state agreed not to seek "the death penalty." The best offer from the state was that if Mary pled guilty, the state would agree to fifteen years in prison. Winkler's defense team declined the offer. The trial started in April 2007 in the courtroom of Judge Weber McCraw in the district court of McNairy County, Tennessee. After the questioning of potential jurors, Judge McCraw swore in a panel of twelve jurors (ten women and two men) to hear the evidence in the case. The state, having the burden of proof, presented several witnesses including investigating officers, the medical examiner, and forensic experts to prove their case. Law enforcement personnel indicated that Mary Winkler admitted repeatedly that she killed Matthew during the early morning hours of March 22, 2006. The murder weapon was a twelve-gauge shotgun that belonged to the victim. Winkler admitted that she shot her husband in the back as he lay sleeping in bed. The prosecution introduced into evidence, a twelve-gauge shotgun that was seized from Mary Winkler's vehicle as she was arrested in Orange Beach, Alabama. The shotgun was identified by the state's witnesses as the murder weapon that was used to kill Matthew Winkler on March 22, 2006. The state rested its case against Mary Winkler. The defense counsel made a motion to dismiss the charge of murder against his client on the grounds that there was insufficient evidence to support the state's charge of murder in the first degree. The evidence presented indicated that proper charge in the case should be manslaughter, not murder. Judge McCraw overruled the defense motion.

The Defense Case

The evidence presented by the defense did not dispute that basic fact that Mary Winkler had shot her husband in the back while he was sleeping. The defense focused on the issue of "conflicts" in the Winkler marriage. Witnesses testified that Mary was the victim of "spousal abuse"! Dan Freeman, Mary's father, testified that on several occasions he observed his daughter had bruises on her hands, arms, and face. No amount of makeup could cover up her physical injuries. Mary would deny that Matt had beaten her. Freeman stated that during the last three years, Mary's injuries happened more frequently. Several personal friends of Mary testified that she would show up at church and other public places with visible bruises. On one occasion, Mary showed up at a church function with a huge "black eye"!

Mary took the witness stand and told the jury about the "marital conflicts" that she had in her marriage to Matthew. Mary wanted to get a divorce, but Matt repeatedly told her that divorce was out of the question for a minister; it would ruin his career as a preacher! Mary said there were money issues in the marriage. The couple's bank account was messed up and overdrawn by several thousand dollars. Matt blamed their financial chaos on Mary's mismanagement of the family finances. Matthew also had "weird demands" in the bedroom. He wanted to do "unnatural sex acts," and he wanted her to dress up in "slutty clothing," wear a kinky wig, and eight-inch-high heels, just like a "street hooker"! Defense counsel introduced into evidence: the clothing, the wig, and the high heels that her husband demanded that she wear in their bedroom. In conclusion, the defense presented evidence from the minister's computer, showing that it contained "porn films" that Matt forced Mary to watch at night.

The defense counsel for Mary Winkler concluded its case by calling an "expert witness," Dr. Lynne Zager, a clinical psychologist who testified that she had several sessions with Mary Winkler over a period of six months prior to the trial. Based on her counseling sessions with Mary, Dr. Zager testified that, in her professional opinion, Mary had been the victim of "spousal abuse" over a period of several years. In her expert opinion, Mary suffered from a condition known as "post-traumatic stress syndrome"! Mary was experiencing mental depression after years of spousal abuse. The defense rested its case, and the judge recessed the trial to review jury instructions that would be given to the jury prior to their deliberations. During the review in the judge's chambers, the defense advocated that the evidence supported several different possible verdicts. Judge McCraw reviewed the evidence and concluded that the jury should be given instructions on first-degree murder, second-degree murder, and manslaughter. Closing arguments were presented by the state's attorney.

The state prosecutor reviewed the evidence, telling the jury that Mary Winkler had planned to kill her husband in order to extricate herself from a difficult and troubled marriage. Mary Winkler killed her husband with a twelve-gauge shotgun while he was asleep in his bed.

The defense countered with its evidence that Mary Winkler was the victim of "spousal abuse" by a husband who was physically and mentally abusive over a period of several years. After the closing arguments, the jury retired and deliberated for a period of more than eight hours. The jury returned with a surprising verdict: Mary Winkler was guilty of the lesser charge of "voluntary manslaughter." The jury was discharged, and the judge set the case for judgment and sentencing for June 8, 2007.

Mary Winkler's Punishment

At the sentencing hearing on June 8, 2007, evidence was presented that Mary Winkler had no prior criminal record and that she was eligible for a possible sentence with a range of punishment from three to years in prison on a conviction of voluntary manslaughter.

Each side was allowed to present "victim's impact statements" about the crime and the defendant. The sentencing hearing lasted more than five hours. At the conclusion of the evidence, Judge McCraw stated that he had received more than ninety letters from citizens around the country. Reviewing the evidence, Judge McCraw concluded that Mary Winkler should be given a sentence of three years, with two years and five months of the sentence to be suspended upon her good behavior. The judge further ordered that Mary be given credit for time served in the county jail awaiting trial, some 143 days. The judge stated that in the final analysis, the defendant should spend sixty-seven days in a mental health facility for the treatment of her mental health issues. Mary Winkler was to be released from custody in August 2007. The courtroom and the community were shocked by the lenient sentence of the court. Afterward, one of the members of the jury, a man, stated that the jury verdict was based on gender discrimination in the criminal justice process. The majority of the jury (ten women) wanted to give Mary Winkler "leniency" in the face of the "spousal abuse" since she had suffered through many years of living with husband, Matthew Winkler. Mary Winkler completed her sentence and released from custody on August 15,

2007. Eventually, Mary regained custody of her three children, and she lives a quiet, obscure life in the country for the last several years.

Analysis of the Mary Winkler Case

An examination of the facts of the Winkler case indicate that a jury composed of ten ladies and two men in the community concluded that there was clear evidence of "spousal abuse" by the victim, Matt Winkler, prior to the date of the murder. The jury panel elected to convict her of the lesser crime of "manslaughter" based upon Mary's history of being the "real victim" in the case. The trial judge imposed a final sentence that indicated that some leniency be given to Mary Winkler based on her evidence of "spousal abuse," hence the punishment of only seven months in jail with the balance of a three-year sentence to be suspended. The fact that Mary Winkler only spent sixty-seven days in jail following her conviction for the murder of her husband reflects the evolving standards in the American criminal justice system with regard to the treatment of women that have been the victims of "spousal abuse"! More and more jurisdictions recognize the concept of the "battered women's syndrome" and have allowed the defense counsel to present evidence about the marital history of the parties involved in the case.

THE MILLIONAIRE KILLER
Virginia v. Susan Cummings (1997)

Susan Cummings was born in Monte Carlo, Monaco, on July 21, 1962. Susan was the daughter of Samuel Cummings, a wealthy arms dealer who had made several billion dollars in the international arms market. The Cummings family moved to the United States in the 1970s. Samuel bought a lavish ranch containing over two thousand acres near the town of Warrenton, Virginia. The property was renamed Ashland Farms. Susan inherited the property after her father died. Susan eventually sold the ranch for $4.9 million and purchased a smaller ranch that contained over a thousand acres. Susan had a great love of horses and acquired several dozen horses over the next few years. Susan loved to ride her horses over her thousand-acre ranch. Susan would attend public events relating to horses over the entire state of Virginia.

Roberto Villegas was born in poverty in a rural area of Argentina. Roberto's only escape from his impoverished life was his love of horses. Roberto loved to ride horses and became involved in playing polo during his teenage years. Roberto's agility on a horse soon became recognized by officials with the Argentine polo team. Roberto signed on with the team and soon became the best player on the team. The Argentine polo team competed in several international competitions including the United States. Roberto eventually was able to immigrate to the United States, settling in Florida in 1991. Within three years, Roberto was playing on a polo team that would play matches in Atlantic states including the state of Virginia. Roberto met Susan Cummings at a polo training facility in Fauquier County, Virginia, in 1995. It appeared to be love at first sight!

The Willow Run polo training school, outside Warrenton, Virginia, covers several hundred acres filled with lush green meadows, large willow trees, and a beautiful stream flowing through the middle of the acreage. In the 1990s, the school was operated by Jean Marie Turon. Mr. Turon became familiar with Roberto as a rising star on the national polo circuit. Turon invited Roberto to visit the school. Impressed with the facilities, Roberto inquired whether he could work there during the off-season. Turon agreed, asking him to help with the training the students who were enrolling during the current term of the school.

In the summer of 1995, a shy, slender attractive lady enrolled at the school. Her name: Susan Cummings. Over the period of the next several months, a romantic relationship developed between Susan and Roberto. In addition to weekly polo lessons, the couple would go out to lunch. Weeks later, the couple would go out to dinner at elegant restaurants in Warrenton, Virginia. During the fall of 1995, Roberto would spend weekends at the Cummings horse ranch.

Roberto, being tired of being on the road and attending polo events up and down the East Coast of the United States, wanted to get a stable job. Susan offered him the job of being the "foreman" of her large horse ranch. Roberto agreed and moved into the "guesthouse" on the ranch during the summer of 1996. Susan lived her large mansion, two hundred yards away. Sometimes, Roberto would stay overnight with Susan in her mansion. Roberto was good at running the ranch and taking care of the horses. Susan was very happy with the arrangement. Roberto loved the quiet and peaceful atmosphere of the Virginia countryside and working with the horses.

While Susan was generous with regard to operating her horse ranch, she was an old "tightwad" with regard to paying Roberto a reasonable monthly salary. Roberto wanted more money. She refused. The tense feelings between the couple increased as the spring of 1997 approached. Roberto was weary of being on the road again, traveling the polo circuit. He asked Susan for more money to offset his loss of income from the polo matches. Roberto asked for her hand in marriage. Susan was unsure what she should do. While she enjoyed all the benefits of having Roberto running her horse ranch, she was very reluctant to mix business with pleasure. It could turn out to be "a disaster"! Susan did not want to make a commitment, considering her extensive wealth and real estate holdings. The tension escalated between the couple in the summer of 1997. Roberto became increasingly upset with Susan about their personal relationship. Roberto wanted answers about their future. Would they be together forever? Susan kept refusing his demands for an answer!

Roberto would become extremely upset and threaten Susan with physical violence. On August 20, 1997, after another violent outburst from Roberto, Susan went to the Fauquier County Sheriff's Office to try and get "a restraining order" against Roberto. Susan, in her statement to the sheriff's office, stated, "In the last six months, he has begun to show sign of aggression toward me." She continued in her statement, saying, "He has threatened to kill me, saying that he was going to shoot me in the head." Susan told the sheriff's department that Roberto had threatened to drown her in the bathtub and make it look like an accident. Susan described Roberto as being "short-fused" and "acting crazy." What should she do?

The sheriff's office advised Susan to file a complaint with the county magistrate and get a restraining order against Villegas. Before leaving the sheriff's office, Susan was able to schedule an appointment to see the magistrate on September 8, 1997, and get the restraining order.

The Day of the Murder (September 7, 1997)

At approximately 8:50 a.m. of September 7, 1997, a call was placed to 911 for Fauquier County, Virginia. The operator answered, "Nine, one, one emergency! What is your emergency?"

A woman's voice on the line stated, "A man has been shot at my house. Please send help immediately!"

The operator replied, "What happened?"

The woman responded, "He came at me with a knife! I had to shoot him!" Continuing, the woman stated, "Please send help. I think that he is dying!"

The operator inquired, "What is your location?"

In a calm voice, the woman stated, "This is Susan Cummings. My house is located at Ashland Farms, just outside of town."

The operator concluded, "Help is on the way. They should be there in twenty minutes!" Susan hung up the phone and immediately called her family attorney. Recognizing the serious nature of a homicide investigation and possible criminal charges against his client, her attorney immediately called the best criminal defense lawyer in the state of Virginia: Blair Howard. Howard agreed to assist in the matter and traveled out to Cummings ranch. The grounds of Ashland Farms were swarming with sheriff's cars as Howard drove up to the large ranch house, arriving at approximately 10:30 a.m.

Entering the house, Howard identified himself and asked to speak to his client, Susan Cummings. Howard was ushered into room where Cummings was sitting. Howard asked to speak with his client alone. A sheriff's deputy directed them to an adjoining room. Howard looked at Susan and noticed that she had raw cuts and red slashes on her wrists. Howard also observed blood running down the sides of her arms. Howard was advised that a sheriff's deputy had taken several photos of her arms and hands. Susan related to Howard what had happened in the kitchen that morning. While Susan was talking to her attorney, a forensics team was searching the crime scene to collect any items that could be used in a possible criminal case related to the shooting of Roberto Villegas. A representative of the coroner's office verified that Villegas was dead, and the body was removed from the crime scene and taken to the coroner's office for an autopsy. Cummings was asked to give a statement the sheriff's officer. Cummings declined to talk, based on the advice of her attorney, Blair Howard. Sheriff's deputies arrested Susan and transported her to the Fauquier County Sheriff's Office for booking into the county jail. Blair Howard followed Susan to the sheriff's office.

On September 10, 1997, Susan cummings was officially charged with the crime of first-degree murder in the district court of Fauquier County, Virginia. Appearing before the judge, Attorney Blair Howard waived reading of the formal complaint and entered a plea of "*not guilty*" on behalf of Susan Cummings. Defense counsel asked for a show-cause hearing immediately. The hearing was set for ten days later, and Susan Cummings was released from jail after posting an appearance bond of $75,000.

On November 24, 1996, the Fauquier County grand jury formally issued an indictment charging Susan Cummings with the crime of the first-degree murder of Roberto Villegas on September 7, 1997. The case was set for a jury trial on the spring docket, May 1998. The trial started on May 4, 1998. After summoning in the prospective members to serve on the jury panel, the trial judge allowed the prosecutors and the defense counsel to question the prospective jurors about their qualifications to serve on the jury. After a full day of inquiry, a jury panel of eight women and four men were sworn in to serve as jurors in the case. The state presented evidence from deputies of the Fauquier County Sheriff's Office related to their investigation and findings at the crime scene. Pictures were presented showing the victim, Roberto Villegas, lying on the kitchen floor of Cummings's house in a pool of blood. A ballistics expert identified the murder weapon as a pistol that matched a gun that belonged to the defendant, Susan Cummings. An expert witness from the coroner's office testified that the death of Roberto Villegas was the result of four shots fired at close range, a distance less than six feet away. An audiotape of the 911 call made to the sheriff's office was played in court. Character witnesses called by the state indicated that Roberto was a nice young man who had developed a very close personal relationship with Susan Cummings. According to his friends, Roberto was "in love" with Susan and he wanted them to get married and have kids. The prosecutors argued that the case was clearly a first-degree murder case and that Susan Cummings should be sentenced to a term of "life imprisonment" without parole.

The Defense of Susan Cummings

The defense attorney hired by Susan Cummings was one of the most prominent criminal defense lawyers in the state of Virginia. Dark Howard had gained national attention in his successful defense of Lorena Bobbitt in the early 1990s. The focus of the defense of Cummings centered on the "violent character" of Roberto Villegas.

Evidence from ten years earlier indicated that Villegas was charged with "assault and battery" by another woman. The defense also presented testimony from several witnesses that Villegas was belligerent and abusive toward them. An additional factor in the defense was that Cummings had a fundamental "right to defend herself" when she was attacked in her own home. The state of Virginia had recognized the Castle Rule for more than fifty years. Under the Castle Rule doctrine, a person has a right to protect themselves in their own home if the person is in "imminent danger" of personal harm by an intruder entering into the premises. Taking the witness stand, Cummings testified in her own defense. Cummings told the jury that on the morning of September 7, 1997, Roberto Villegas came into her home uninvited and started threatening her. Cummings told him to leave the house. Villegas refused and approached her with a knife in his right hand. Cummings and Villegas struggled, and Villegas slashed her with his knife. During the struggle, Cummings pulled out a gun from a drawer and fired it at Villegas. A total of four shots were fired before Villegas fell to the floor and passed out. Cummings immediately dialed 911 and asked for help.

Additional evidence was presented by the defense relating to the personal injuries that Cummings suffered to her arms and hands as a result of being attacked by the knife that Villegas pulled out when he entered the house. Photos of Susan Cummings arms and hands taken at the crime scene were admitted into evidence. The photos revealed several cuts and abrasions on Susan's arms and hands. A copy of the offense report filed by Cummings at the sheriff's office on August 27, 1997, was also admitted into evidence. The defense completed their presentation of evidence and rested their case. On rebuttal, the state called a crime scene analyst, Robert Zinn. Mr. Zinn testified that an examination of the knife, lying beside Roberto's body, had almost no blood on it. This scientific finding would indicate that Roberto did not have the knife in his hand at the time that he was shot.

The implication of this scientific finding was that the knife was placed near Roberto's hand after he was shot. After the rebuttal evidence was concluded, the court gave legal instructions to the members of the jury. The jury was directed to consider several possible verdicts. The directions allowed the jury to determine if Susan Cummings had committed (1) the crime of murder, first degree; (2) the crime of murder, second degree; (3) the crime of manslaughter, first degree; (4) the crime of manslaughter, second degree; and (5) the finding that Susan Cummings had not committed any of these crimes. In that event, the judge instructed the jury to return a verdict of "*not guilty*" on all charges. The jury retired and started their deliberations. The jury deliberated for a period of eight hours over two days. On May 13, 1998, the jury returned to court with its verdict.

The Jury Verdict

The jury verdict delivered in court was, "We the jury, duly sworn to hear the evidence and render a verdict, find as follows: that the defendant is guilty of the crime of the manslaughter, and we affix her punishment at sixty days in jail and a fine of $2,500."

The parties and the spectators in the courtroom were shocked at the jury verdict. The judge dismissed the jury and set sentencing for May 14, 1998. Susan Cummings appeared before the court and told the judge, through her defense counsel Clark Howard, that she accepted the verdict of the jury and that she would not appeal her conviction. The court ordered Cummings to begin serving her sentence immediately. Cummings was remanded to the custody of the sheriff of Fauquier County and served her sentence. The entire cell block of the jail where Cummings was confined was cleared out so that Cummings could serve her sentence in a quiet, peaceful environment. Cummings was allowed a "special large cell" and had a phone placed in her jail cell to use at her convenience. Cummings was also allowed "unlimited visitation" by friends and relatives of the family. Cummings was released from custody after only fifty-seven days with time off for good behavior. Subsequently, the family of Roberto Villegas filed a "wrongful death action" against Susan Cummings in the district court of Fauquier County, Virginia. The family sought damages of more than $15 million from Cummings. The case was settled, out of court, for an undisclosed amount in 2005. Susan

Cummings continues to live a quiet, secret life on her large horse farm in Fauquier County, Virginia, today.

An Analysis of the Cummings Case

The jury verdict in the Cummings case raises several questions. Why would a jury find her guilty of the least possible charge, manslaughter, and assess her punishment at only sixty days in jail? Did Susan Cummings, a very rich woman worth several million dollars, escape any significant punishment because of her wealth and influence? Do the "rich get off" while the "poor" go to jail? There are several factors to consider:

1. Susan Cummings did use her wealth and money to hire one of the best criminal defense attorneys in the United States in the person of Blair Howard. Mr. Howard's trial strategy obviously influenced the jury to assess the facts in a light most favorable to Susan Cummings and return a very lenient punishment against her.

2. The character and background of the victim, Roberto Villegas, may have played a role in influencing the jury to render a verdict that was very favorable to the defendant. The police and court records of Roberto's actions prior to the date of the murder may have been a factor in influencing the jury in its verdict.

3. The assertion of the defense in asserting the Castle Rule may have been a factor in the jury's decision. A home owner such as Susan Cummings does have the right to use "deadly force" against an intruder that would pose a threat and an "imminent danger" to the home owner's safety.

4. The composition of the jury may have been a factor. There were eight women and only four men on the jury panel. The majority of the panel composed of eight women was more likely to have sympathy for a woman facing an intruder who was trying to kill her.

THE HUSBAND FROM HELL
Texas v. Charlene Hill (2006)

Charlene was first introduced to Danny Hill by a mutual friend in 1979. Charlene had recently gone through a difficult divorce in dissolving her first marriage and had basically given up on finding another mate for a while. After dating for several months, Charlene accepted Danny's proposal to get married. The couple wed in 1981 and moved into a small rental house in a suburb of Houston, Texas. Since Darlene had a small child from her first marriage, Danny allowed her to be a stay-at-home mom while he continuing to work in the landscaping business. The Hills were graced with the birth of a son whom they named Jeremy.

Two years later, Charlene gave birth to a beautiful young girl that they named Joby. The Hills decided to set up their own landscaping business. Darlene agreed to serve as the secretary, bookkeeper, and manager of the business while Danny would supervise the labor force. The landscaping business thrived, and Danny was able to add a dozen employees over the next ten years. By 2000, the Hill Landscaping Company had fifty employees and gross revenues of over $ 5 million per year.

The Hill family was very active and adventurous. During time off from work, Danny and Charlene would take their kids on "camping" and "fishing" trips. The kids enjoyed the outdoors and being dose to nature. Eventually, Danny decided to purchase some real estate near the Brazos River and move his business down by the river. The Hills also built a large home on an acreage adjacent to the river. Life was blooming for the Hill family. Danny Hill continued expanding his business enterprises, constructing multiple storage facilities in and around southern Houston. Darlene enjoyed the luxury of being a "stay-at-home" mom while continuing to manage the finances of the landscaping business. Sadly, a tragedy caused the Hill family to disintegrate to chaos, discontent, and, ultimately, *murder*!

The Motorcycle Accident (August 9, 2003)

The income from the Hill Landscaping business allowed Charlene and Danny Hill to enjoy the luxuries of life. One of Danny's favorite pastime was to travel throughout the Texas Hill country on his Harley-Davidson motorcycle. On many occasions, Charlene would ride on the back of Danny's motorcycle. On a warm August day, the Hills were out for an evening ride on their motorcycle when Danny suddenly lost control of the cycle and skidded down into a ravine. Charlene suffered a severe injury to her left leg as a result of the accident. Danny sustained a massive head injury and a "brain concussion." Charlene had to undergo surgery to repair her injured leg. Danny was hospitalized in "intensive care" for a period of three weeks. The accident caused a significant "personality change" in Danny. While he was able to return to work a few months later, he became increasingly hostile toward his employees and his family members. Charlene tried to pacify Danny when his angry moods became more hostile. Arguments between the couple escalated into physical violence with Danny punching and kicking Charlene during the arguments. Danny also showed increased violence toward their two boys, striking and hitting them when he got upset with their behavior. At one point, Charlene took the kids and left the house, going to California to live with relatives. After ten months of separation, the couple agreed to a reconciliation conditioned upon Danny agreeing to undergo mental health counseling and anger management therapy to deal with his anger issues. Charlene moved back to Texas with the children. Danny attended a few sessions of mental health counseling when he decided that it was a waste of time and money. The conflicts in their marriage reappeared with daily arguments. The arguments escalated into physical violence with Danny slapping Charlene and whipping the kids for no apparent reason. Danny threatened to kill Charlene if she tried to leave.

The Day of the Murder (November 14, 2006)

After Charlene and Danny reconciled in 2004, Charlene was forced on several occasions to deal with Danny and his violent behavior. On one occasion, she took the kids to school and came back home to pack their belongings in suitcases and prepared to leave Danny again.

Danny came back to the residence and caught Charlene packing up to leave. Danny exploded, punching and slapping Charlene. Danny tied Charlene up to a chair in the garage and told her that he was going to pour gasoline on her and set her on fire if she ever tried to leave him again. Charlene, fearing for the safety of her children, assured Danny that she would never try to leave ever again. A few months later, Danny became enraged and hit Charlene with a kitchen chair.

She was forced to seek medical attention at a nearby hospital. On another occasion, Charlene locked Danny out of the bedroom. Danny retrieved a gun from his work truck and fired several shots into the bedroom door. Law enforcement officers responded to the residence. Charlene was advised that Danny would be arrested and taken to jail if she was willing to sign a formal "citizen's complaint." Charlene refused to sign the complaint, fearing that Danny would kill her when he got out of jail. On the morning of November 14, 2006, Danny left the residence and headed to work at his landscape business. While working, Danny received a call from his brother, asking him to come over to the storage facilities to resolve a dispute with a tenant. Danny got into a verbal confrontation with the tenant that resulted in the police being called to resolve the dispute. Danny was very angry with his brother's handling of the matter. That evening, he came home in a "very angry mood"! Charlene could see that she was in for a difficult evening. Charlene and Danny got into verbal argument in their bedroom. Charlene pulled a pistol out of the nightstand and pointed it at Danny. She fired three shots. *Bam! Bam! Bam!* Danny collapsed onto the floor and died immediately!

The Law Enforcement Investigation

Charlene rushed to the phone and called 911, requesting an ambulance. Paramedics arrived twenty minutes later and transported Danny to a hospital in Houston, Texas. Law enforcement questioned Charlene at the scene, asking what had had happened. Charlene told the police that she was forced to shoot Danny in self-defense after the couple got into a verbal argument in the bedroom of their family home. Charlene was arrested and taken to the county jail in Fort Bend, Texas. The sheriff's office of Fort Bend presented the results of its investigation to the district attorney of Fort Bend County. Subsequently, evidence was presented to a Texas grand jury panel which issued an official indictment against Charlene Hill, charging her with the crime of *"first-degree murder"*! Charlene entered a plea of *"not guilty"* and requested a trial by jury. Charlene selected a well-known criminal defense attorney, George Parnham, to represent her in the trial. Since the state was not seeking the death penalty, the court allowed Charlene to be released from jail, upon posting an appearance bond of $1 million.

The Trial-Texas V. Charlene Hill

The murder case of *Texas v. Charlene Hill* finally came on for a jury trial in September 2009, a delay of almost three years after the homicide. The state presented its evidence, focusing on the facts of the shooting and Charlene's admission that she shot and killed her husband on the evening of November 14, 2006. The prosecutor told the jury that the motive for the murder was money! Charlene and Danny were millionaires, and Charlene wanted to take it all and get rid of Danny!

The Evidence for the Defendant Charlene Hill

The defense of Charlene Hill was predicated on the theory that Charlene was forced to shoot Danny Hill in "self-defense"! The defense presented medical records dating back to the motorcycle accident showing that the victim, Danny Hill, had suffered a "brain concussion" as a result of the accident and that his personality completely changed following the accident. Additional evidence including police reports disclosing several instances where the law enforcement was called to the Hill residence after calls to 911 in Houston, Texas. While Charlene refused to sign a formal "citizen's complaints," the reports noted the evidence of physical injuries to Charlene.

Records from the "Texas Child Protective Services Office" indicated that the children of Danny Hill had been injured as the result of physical assaults by Danny Hill. Several friends of the family testified that they observed physical injuries to the head, neck, and face of Charlene after being assaulted by Danny Hill. Charlene took the witness stand on her own behalf and described the various instances of spousal abuse by Danny Hill during her twenty-year marriage to Danny. Charlene detailed the various instances when she tried to leave. Each time, Danny Hill would stop her and beat her, telling her that he was "going to kill her" if she ever tried to leave him again. The defense presented expert testimony that Charlene was a clear example of "the battered women's syndrome." The defense rested their case, and the judge gave detailed instructions to the jury. The judge advised the jurors to retire and began their deliberations. The jury panel deliberated for more than twelve hours over two days. The jurors were "deadlocked" and could not agree on a verdict. A "mistrial" was declared by the judge. The case would have to be tried before a different judge and jury at some date in the future.

The Second Trial for Charlene Hill (January 2011)

The second trial for Charlene Hill started in January, 2011. The state presented the same basic evidence that it had presented in the first trial. The motive for the murder of Danny Hill was clearly who should have control of all the money and real estate assets that the Hills had acquired during their twenty-five years of marriage and business dealings together.

The prosecutor asserted that Charlene wanted it all for herself! The state prosecutors even forced two of Charlene's children to testify about the fights that occurred between their mother and their father. The purpose of their testimony was to show to the jury that their mother instigated most of the fights by her verbal abuse toward her husband. Why would her grown children testify against their own mother? If Charlene was convicted in the murder of Danny Hill, she would be legally excluded, under Texas law, from receiving any inheritance from the estate, thereby allowing the kids to inherit the entire estate! Amazing what people will do for money! Send their own mother to prison for the rest of her life!

The defense of Charlene Hill presented the same evidence that given in the first trial: that the shooting of Danny Hill on November 14, 2006, was "justifiable homicide"! That Charlene was forced to shoot her husband when he started to assault her when he got home from work. At the conclusion of the defense evidence, the judge gave instructions to the jury on the evidence that had been presented and the right of "self-defense" under the law of Texas.

The jury retired and began their deliberations in the case. Several hours passed with no verdict! Why? Was the second jury deadlocked in the same manner as the first jury? What would happen to Charlene Hill? Was she guilty or not guilty of the crime of murder?

Charlene Hill Decided to Enter a Plea of Guilty

The jury had been deliberating for several hours with no apparent verdict in sight. The prosecutor started discussions with the defense counsel about a possible resolution to the case. The state wanted to avoid another mistrial if the jury was deadlocked and unable to reach a verdict. The defense also wanted to avoid a possible third trial but also wanted to avoid the possibility of Charlene being sent to prison for an extended period of time. At approximately 6:30 p.m., the attorneys for both sides and Charlene appeared before the judge. Charlene elected to withdraw her plea of not guilty and enter a "plea of guilty" in exchange for a recommended sentence of leniency from the judge. The judge, as the plea agreement was being announced by the respective parties, was notified by the bailiff that the jury had reached a verdict. District Judge James Shoemake was faced with a legal dilemma! What should the judge do? Accept the plea agreement or allow the jury to return to the courtroom and announce their verdict. Judge Shoemake elected to accept the plea agreement! The jury was summoned back into the courtroom and advised that the case had been resolved. The judge thanked the jury for their service and allowed them to leave the courthouse. The court concluded the hearing on the plea agreement, announcing that the court accepted the plea agreement. The Texas court ordered that Charlene Hill be given "a deferred adjudication" for a period of ten years. No jail time! Charlene had to complete five years of probation, with no violations of the law. Charlene walked out of the Fort Bend County Courthouse after a legal nightmare of more than four years. Charlene completed the terms of the plea agreement and allowed to return a quiet life after thirty years of violence and abuse.

The Charlene Hill case is a difficult case to analyze in many respects. While Danny and Charlene had a successful business that generated millions of dollars over the twenty-five years that they were married, their personal lives were often chaotic. Money does not always bring happiness! Charlene may have controlled the money, but Danny controlled the relationship, putting her in constant fear of "spousal abuse" when he lost his temper. The events leading up to the killing of Danny Hill on November 14, 2006, can be interpreted in two different ways: Was the murder of Danny Hill caused by greed—Charlene wanted to take all the money and get rid of her husband of twenty-five years? Or was the killing of Danny Hill a case of "self-defense," after years of spousal abuse? Two different jury panels in two different trials had to decide those issues. Apparently, the evidence was so conflicting that neither jury panel could agree on the proper verdict. Since the burden in a criminal case is on the state to prove Charlene Hill's guilt beyond a reasonable doubt, it is clear that the jury panel could not find Charlene Hill guilty of the charges. The plea disposition by the Texas court, allowing Charlene Hill to go free without a jail sentence, was quite controversial! The relatives of Danny Hill complained that Charlene should have been sent to jail for at least twenty years. Charlene agreed to plead guilty in exchange for no jail time in order to get the legal nightmare over! Charlene

Hill, after completing her ten years of probation, was allowed to go free with no criminal conviction on her record. The saddest part of the Charlene Hill case is the state of Texas forcing Charlene's children to testify against her in the murder trial. While two of the children did, in fact, testify in the case, the third child, Joby, did not testify! He committed "suicide" prior to court hearing, saying that he could not live with himself if he was forced to take the witness stand and testify against his mother, Charlene! A "sad case" with a "sad ending."

THE CASE OF THE
BURNING BED
Michigan v. Francine Hughes (1977)

Francine Hughes was born on August 17, 1947, in Stockbridge, Michigan, the beautiful daughter of Walter Moran and his wife, Hazel. Walter was a farm laborer, working on farms, harvesting crops (primarily onions). The small house that the Francine's family lived was furnished by Walter's employer. The house had two bedrooms and "no bathroom"! The living conditions were very crude. Francine's mom, Hazel, was a stay-at-home mom, a very submissive wife to her husband, Walter. Francine went to school in an old two-room schoolhouse, typical in rural America during the 1940s. Walter would work in the fields all day, come home, eat supper with the family, and then head to bed by 8:00 p.m.

On weekends, Walter would get drunk on Friday and stay drunk all weekends. Generally, on Saturday nights, he would play cards and get drunk with the boys. Francine's mother, Hazel, would complain; and Walter would beat her up and tell her to "shut up and go to bed." Walter got arrested and thrown in jail for stealing tools from his place of employment to have pocket money to go drinking and gambling! Francine's homelife was a "living nightmare" that she wanted to escape from as soon as possible. She did not want to "go home" after school. Francine was looking for an escape out the "nightmare"!

The answer to her prayers to escape her "terrible homelife" appeared one evening. Francine attended a school social event and got to meet a young man by the name of Mickey. Mickey asked her out for a date later in the week. Francine gladly accepted. Mickey had a car. Francine could escape her terrible homelife. Heaven had arrived!

After Francine and Mickey had been dating for more than six months, the couple started talking about marriage. Mickey proposed? Francine gladly accepted!

The young couple got married on November 14, 1963. Mickey had just turned eighteen. Francine was only sixteen. Her mother, Hazel, had to sign "a written consent" in order for Francine to get married. During the first few months of their marriage, the couple lived with his parents. Mickey had dropped out of high school and had difficulty finding a job. Francine had dropped out of school as well. Francine took a job as a waitress at a nearby restaurant. Mickey would lie around the house, drinking beer. One day, Mickey got into a fight with his dad. Mickey's mom called the police and had him arrested. Mickey spent a few days in jail. The newlyweds were forced to move out and find a place of their own. Eventually, Mickey found a manual labor job, working in a factory. Mickey forced Francine to quit her job as a waitress. Mickey continuing his habit of drinking every night when he got home from work. After downing a six-pack of beer, Mickey would become angry and find a reason to "slap Francine around"! The fights and the physical beatings of Francine would generally occur two or three times a week. After several months of enduring the violent environment, Francine fled the apartment and went home to live with her mother. Mickey would call and beg to be forgiven. Francine would cave in and return to the apartment they shared. Within a few weeks, the drinking would return and eventually Mickey returned to his old ways of slapping Francine around and beating her up for no apparent reason. Then Francine learned that she was pregnant. Life seemed to be better for Francine.

A beautiful little boy, Jimmy, was born on December 30, 1964. Francine was so happy at becoming a mother. Mickey seemed to change for the better with the new baby. He got new job at General Motors, working on the assembly line in an Oldsmobile plant. Francine soon became pregnant with a second child. Suddenly,

Mickey had a fight with his supervisor at work and quit his job. Mickey decided to follow his brother to Kansas to take a job in construction. Francine followed, moving to Overland Park, Kansas. In a matter of few months, Mickey lost his job, and the family moved to Camden, Missouri. Within six months, Mickey got fired from that job, and the family moved back home, moving in with his mother. After the birth of their second child, Dana, Mickey returned to his old habits of drinking all day and fighting with Francine at night.

Francine, at this point, decided that she had "had enough!" Francine went to the local "legal aid" office and filed for divorce. The divorce was finalized in 1974.

Approximately, six months later, Mickey was involved in horrible auto accident. The car was "totaled out," and Mickey was taken to a medical facility in Ann Arbor, Michigan. Mickey was seriously injured and was in "intensive care" for several days. He slowly recovered. Francine visited with him every day and invited him to live with her after his released from the hospital. Since Mickey suffered from permanent injuries, he could no longer work. Mickey applied for and eventually received disability benefits. With a steady income from the disability benefits, Mickey returned to his old habits of "drinking and fighting" with Francine on a daily basis. The nightmare days of her earlier marriage to Mickey were returning!

Francine was just getting her self-esteem back when Mickey had his auto accident. She had returned to school and got her GED. Francine enrolled in a local business school, hoping to gain a better education and get a good-paying job. Mickey's continuing health problems created a hostile environment for Francine to take care of her children and continue her educational goals.

The Day of the Murder (March 9, 1977)

Francine returned home from school at approximately 4:00 p.m. Mickey was "blind drunk" and mad at Francine for some unknown reason. Francine started to prepare food for her kids' dinner. While she was fixing the meal, Mickey came into the kitchen and started yelling at her. Mickey wanted her to "quit school" and stay home with him. Francine refused, telling Mickey that she was "going to stay in school and complete her degree." Mickey got really upset and set fire to her school textbooks. Mickey started slapping her around in the kitchen. One of the kids called 911 and asked the police to come out to the house. Within twenty minutes, two sheriff's deputies responded to the call. The deputies told the pair, Mickey and Francine, to calm down and quit fighting. An offense report was filled out, and the deputies left the residence. Francine returned to the kitchen and started preparing the evening meal again. Mickey came in and dumped the entire meal on the floor and made Francine clean it up. Francine finally agreed to "quit school" to calm Mickey down. While she fed the kids, Mickey drank a six-pack of beer. After dinner, Mickey forced her into the bedroom, where he raped her. Mickey passed out on the bed. Francine vowed, "I am going to kill you!"

An hour later, Francine put the kids to bed and sat down to watch television. After the kids were asleep, Francine went out into the garage and retrieved a gas can. Francine brought the gas can back into the house and went to the bedroom where Mickey was passed out on the bed. Francine checked on Mickey. He was stone-drunk! Francine took the can of gasoline and sprinkled it around the edges of the bed.

Francine went into the kitchen and got a box of matches. Returning to the bedroom, she struck a match and threw it on the bed. The gasoline quickly ignited, and the bed exploded in a ball of fire. Francine went into the kids' bedroom and got them out of bed. Rounding the kids up, Francine led them out to the car, telling them that they going to have to leave immediately. Francine drove her Ford vehicle down to the Ingham County Sheriff's Department. Francine was confronted by a deputy at the entrance, and she started screaming that she had just killed Mickey and that she had set the house on fire! Francine and the children were escorted into the sheriff's office. Francine repeated her confession. A deputy sheriff was dispatched to the house, and he observed that the entire house was "on fire"! The local fire department was summoned to the house.

It was too late! The house was a total loss. Inside the house, the firemen found the body of Mickey Hughes. The sheriff's office contacted the coroner's office, and the body was removed from the house and taken to the morgue for an autopsy. The cause of death: "smoke inhalation." Francine was interrogated at the sheriff's office and again confessed to setting the house afire and killing her ex-husband. Francine was arrested and placed in the Ingham County Jail. Francine was charged with first-degree murder!

On March 11, 1977, Francine Hughes was arraigned in Ingham District Court. Francine entered a plea of "not guilty" and asked for a court-appointed attorney. A few days later, a local attorney, Aryon Greydanus, was assigned to the case. On March 21, 1997, a show-cause hearing was held in the case. Francine was bound over for trial on two charges: "arson" and "first-degree murder." The judge set the case for trial on the next jury docket. Bail was denied! The state was seeking a sentence of "life imprisonment" on each of the two felony charges. For the next seven months, Francine was confined to the Ingham County Jail awaiting trial. The defense counsel visited with her every week, sometime spending two to three hours with his client. Over the next few months, the defense counsel consulted with several women who lived in the neighborhood where the Hughes family lived. Four ladies living in the area agreed to testify on Francine's behalf, describing the continuing abuse that Francine suffered at the hands of Mickey Hughes. Mr. Greydanus also convinced the judge to order a psychological evaluation of Francine to ascertain her mental state. Dr. Arnold Berkman was retained to examine Francine and evaluate her mental state. Dr. Beckman spent six hours with Francine on the initial visit. Dr. Berkman found no evidence of "psychosis" but did determine that Francine had a severe "neurosis" based on the mental and physical abuse that she had suffered at the hands of Mickey Hughes for a period of more than ten years. Dr. Berkman concluded, in his report that Francine suffered a "mental breakdown" on the date of March 9, 1977. The period of "temporary insanity" concluded when Francine killed her husband by setting fire to the bed that he was passed out drunk and unable to leave. Francine fled the house with the children and immediately turned herself in to the police.

The jury trial for Francine Hughes was scheduled to start on October 17, 1977. On the date of the trial, the assigned judge, Judge Harrison, suddenly disqualified himself, stating that he could not preside over the trial. The case was reassigned to the presiding judge, Roy Hotchkiss. The case was rescheduled for October 24, 1977. The first day of the trial was reserved for "jury selection." During the "voir dire" process, the judge questioned each prospective jury member to determine their qualifications to serve on the jury. Both the state and the defense counsel were allowed to question the jury panel. At the end of the day, a jury panel of two men and ten women were selected to serve on the jury. The state presented its evidence, calling several members of the Ingham County Sheriff's Office to testify. Deputy Steve Schlachter testified that he responded to the 911 call made at the Hughes residence on the afternoon of March 9. Upon confronting Mickey Hughes at the residence, he told the couple to "calm down" and quit fighting. As he was leaving, Schlachter heard Hughes tell Francine that she would pay for calling the cops and that he was going to kill her if she ever called the cops again. Several other deputies testified about the evening of March 9 when Francine came to the sheriff's office and confessed to killing Mickey by setting the bed on fire in her house. Flossie Hughes, Mickey's mother, was called to testify. On cross-examination, Flossie was forced to acknowledge that Mickey would get drunk and slap Francine around. Flossie also admitted that on one occasion, Mickey got drunk and assaulted her. The police were called, and Mickey was arrested and taken to jail for assaulting his own mother! Mickey was released after serving nine days in jail, and Mickey was also ordered to stay away from her house forever!

After four days of trial, the state rested its case. Defense counsel, Greydanus, presented evidence on Francine's behalf. Two of the Hughes children were called to testify. Both kids, Jimmy and Christy, testified that their daddy, Mickey, got drunk almost every day.

Mickey would drink ten to twelve cans of beer each day. When Mickey was completely drunk, he became very abusive toward the kids and Francine. Mickey would "whip" the kids for no apparent reason and slap Francine around at least once a week. Both kids were "scared" of their father. Additional witnesses were called that testified about Mickey's violent behavior, including four women who lived in the neighborhood where the Hughes family lived. Francine took the witness stand and testified in her own behalf. Francine testified that Mickey had a "bipolar personality." One minute, Mickey would a sweet, loving husband. Five minutes later, Mickey would turn into a monster who would slap her and beat her for no apparent reason. On the evening of March 9, 1977, Francine admitted that she "just snapped" and lost total control. After being beaten and raped by Mickey, Francine stated that she went into the garage, retrieved a gas can, and set the bed on fire while Mickey was passed out drunk. Francine testified that as the bedroom was burning, she gathered the kids up and drove down to the sheriff's office. Upon arriving, Francine confessed to the crime and was taken into custody. The defense also presented expert testimony from Dr. Arnold Berkman and Dr. Anne Seidon. Both Dr. Bergman and Dr. Seidon testified that Francine was "mentally ill," suffering from more than ten years of "spousal abuse" at the hands of Mickey Hughes. Dr. Bergman stated that Francine was suffering from "temporary insanity" on March 9, 1977, when she set fire to the bed and burned the house down in order to get away from her abuser, Mickey!

The state was allowed to present "rebuttal evidence" after the defense rested its case. Dr. Roy Blunt was called to testify. Dr. Blunt stated that he examined Francine Hughes at the request of the state's attorney. Dr. Blunt stated that in his professional opinion, Francine was not "mentally ill" on the date in question, March 9, 1977. Dr. Blunt did acknowledge that she had a neurotic disorder on the day of the murder, caused by several years of spousal abuse. In conclusion, Dr. Blunt stated that Francine did not plan to commit the crime, that Francine acted on "impulse," and that the murder was not one of premeditation. The state rested its case. After jury instructions and closing arguments, the case was submitted to the jury for its consideration.

The Jury Verdict

The jury in the Francine Hughes retired to the jury room and began their deliberations at approximately 2:00 p.m. At a little after 7:00, the jury returned to the courtroom with its verdict: "We, the jury, find the defendant, Francine Hughes, *not guilty*, by the reason of "*temporary insanity*." Judge Hotchkiss thanked the jury for their service and excused them from the courtroom. Francine was ordered released from custody as soon as possible. Francine was released from jail the next day and reunited with her children. A few years later, Francine completed her education and became a nurse, working in a nursing home. Francine later remarried and moved to Tennessee. Francine's story and trial were later depicted in 1984 in a highly acclaimed movie starring Farrah Fawcett. The name of the movie: *The Burning Bed.*

Analysis of the Francine Hughes Case

Why would a jury find Francine Hughes not guilty on the charge of arson and first-degree murder? There are several issues raised in the case that may have been factors in the jury decision:

1. The state prosecutor filed a charge of first-degree murder against Francine and sought a term of life imprisonment. Examining the facts and circumstances surrounding the case, did the prosecutor go overboard in filing the first-degree murder charge? Considering the history of violence the victim had with the defendant, a less serious charge of manslaughter would have been more appropriate in the case. This case could be categorized as one as an "overzealous prosecutor" seeking the wrong charge and excessive punishment.

2. The composition of the jury composed of ten women and two men may have been a factor. The women on the jury appeared to be have a great deal of sympathy for the defendant who had been the victim of "spousal abuse" for more

than ten years. Women can easily relate to a woman experiencing marital problems dealing with a hostile husband. The state may have not done a very good job in questioning the jury panel to determine any preconceived ideas or opinions that the ladies on the jury may have with regard to spousal abuse by a husband.

3. The defense evidence presented by Francine's attorney relating to Francine having mental health issues caused by the mental and physical abuse of her husband, Mickey Hughes. The jury verdict of finding the defendant not guilty by reason of "temporary insanity" indicates that the jury gave great consideration to the expert testimony of Dr. Berkman. The Hughes case established the doctrine of the "battered women's syndrome" defense in the United States. This type of defense of the "battered women's syndrome" is allowed in most states in America.

THE DEATH OF AN
OIL TYCOON
Oklahoma v. Donna Bechtel (1984)

Donna Lee was a newly divorced woman who was enjoying a renewed social life after her divorce from her first husband. Donna went out to dinner one evening with some of her lady friends to a fancy restaurant. During the girls' night out at the restaurant, a gentleman stopped by the table and said hello to the ladies.

Donna was introduced to Ken Bechtel, an oil and gas executive with a large oil company. Donna was impressed by Ken's pleasant smile and warm personality. Over the next few weeks, Donna would see Ken at various restaurants in the area. Ken eventually asked Donna out to dinner, and she accepted. During the course of the evening of their first date, Donna learned that Ken was going through a painful divorce. Donna expressed sympathy with the trauma that Ken was experiencing, revealing to him that she had recently gone through a divorce and that she was experiencing some of the same personal issues that he was going through. After several evenings out on the town, Ken invited Donna to accompany him on an overnight trip out of town. Ken promised to take her out to a dinner theater in Chicago. Donna gladly accepted. The couple spent a very romantic weekend in Chicago.

After the Chicago trip, their relationship took a more serious turn. Ken finally got finished with his nasty divorce. The couple went out to an elegant restaurant to celebrate the occasion. After the dinner, Ken brought out an expensive diamond ring and asked Donna to marry him. Donna accepted. The couple was married on

August 25, 1983. The marriage appeared to be "a marriage made in heaven." Appearances can be deceiving! Within a fifteen months, Ken was dead inside his own home. Donna was charged with the crime of first-degree murder.

An Abusive Husband

Kenneth Bechtel was a very exceptional oil and gas executive who had experienced amazing success during the oil boom in the 1970s and the 1980s. However, when the "oil boom" collapsed in the mid-1980s, Ken suffered his share of setbacks, both financially and personally. Most of the oil and gas exploration activity had come to an "abrupt halt." Ken suffered heavy financial losses during the slow down. In his personal life, Ken had similar issues. Ken's wife filed for divorce, seeking one-half of all of his assets. Endless court hearings over financial issues related to the divorce caused Ken to turn to "the bottle" to relieve some of the stress from his personal and professional life. Donna Lee met Ken during this turbulent period of time in his life. While the social consumption of alcohol is a part of life, Donna Lee did not discover the problems that Ken had with alcohol until after their marriage in the summer of 1983. A couple of drinks after work every day is "the norm" in many marital relationships. In the case of Ken Bechtel, a night of heavy drinking was the normal process of relieving stress after a long day at work. Ken would consume usually five to six glasses of whiskey during the evening. Upon getting "totally bombed," Ken would get very abusive. During these episodes, Ken would grab Donna by the hair and slam her into the furniture or a nearby wall. Ken would strike her in the face and chest with a clinched fist. During these episodes of rage, Ken would yell profane obscenities at Donna, calling her "a bitch," "a whore," and "a drunken slut!" Ken would become upset over the untimely death on one of his children who had died several years ago. Drinking heavily would bring back memories of his son. The verbal abuse accelerated to physical violence against Donna. The violence generally consisted of Ken grabbing Donna, throwing her on the floor, and then slapping and beating her for two to three minutes. On three occasions, Donna suffered significant injuries and had to be taken to the emergency room of a nearby hospital. On one occasion, Donna suffered an injury to her neck. The hospital personnel furnished her with a neck collar to wear. On two other occasions, Donna sustained injuries to her head and legs. Concurrent with these visits to the hospital emergency room, Donna would call 911 and request police assistance. On each occasion, Ken was removed from the house and told to stay away.

Ken would later contact Donna and ask for forgiveness and that he be given "another chance." Ken would promise to get help for his issues related to the abuse of alcohol. Donna would make appointments for Ken to see or doctor or a therapist, but Ken would never show up for the appointments. Since Ken was frequently out of town on business trips, Donna would have to call and reschedule the appointments or go to see therapist by herself. It became evident after several missed or cancelled appointments that Ken was never going to get treatment for his problems related to alcohol abuse. Donna felt trapped and considered consulting with an attorney about getting a divorce.

The Day of the Murder (September 23, 1984)

During the early morning hours of September 23, 1984, Ken Bechtel returned home unexpectedly from a business trip. Ken woke up Donna and ordered her to get out of bed and fix him some breakfast. Donna complied with the request and prepared breakfast. Ken slowly ate the breakfast, consuming a couple more shots of whiskey during the meal. Donna headed back up to bed. Ken became upset and told her that he wanted to talk to her. Donna replied that she was "very sleepy" and that she was going back to bed. Upset with this response, Ken grabbed her by her throat and threw her to the floor. Ripping her nightgown off, Ken lifted her up and carried her into the master bedroom. Throwing Donna down on the bed, Ken removed his clothes and proceeded to rape Donna as she lay helpless in the king-size bed.

After satisfying his sexual needs, Ken rolled over and passed out on the other side of the bed. Moving slowly, Donna slowly got out of bed and reached for a cigarette. What should she do? Finally, Donna made her decision. Putting out her cigarette, Donna got out of bed and searched under the bed for what she wanted.

She found it! Moving slowly, Donna reached under the bed and pulled out her .357 Magnum! Donna got to her feet and raised the gun, pointing it toward Ken, who was passed out on the other side of the bed. Donna pulled the trigger on the gun, firing five shots into Ken's back and chest. After checking on him, Donna called 911, asking for the police and medical assistance.

The Trial of Donna Bechtel

Officers with the Edmond Police Department responded to the Bechtel residence on September 23, 1984. Arriving at the scene, the officers assisted medical personnel in loading Ken onto a stretcher for transport to a nearby hospital. An officer inquired of Donna what occurred. Donna was extremely upset and had great difficulty in answering their questions. One officer testified at the trial that Donna had to go to the bathroom several times during the "attempted interview." The officer was so concerned about her medical condition that a second paramedic unit was requested at the residence. The officers testified at trial that Mrs. Bechtel readily admitted to firing the .357-caliber pistol as Ken Bechtel laid in bed sound asleep. After collecting the evidence including the gun at the crime scene, Donna Bechtel was arrested and transported to the Edmond Police Department. Donna was formerly charged with murder in the first degree in the district court of Oklahoma County two days later. After the preliminary hearing, Donna Bechtel was bound over for trial, with the judge setting the case for trial in the spring of 1985. After a very long trial, Donna Bechtel was convicted of first-degree murder and sentenced to a term of life imprisonment without the possibility of parole.

The defendant appealed her conviction to the Oklahoma Court of Criminal Appeals. On June 10, 1987, the appellate court reversed

Bechtel's conviction and remanded the case for a new trial. The reason: "improper exclusion of evidence" related to the legal question of whether Donna Bechtel had waived her Miranda rights and gave a confession.

Donna's Bechtel's Second Trial

The second trial of Donna Bechtel was conducted in Oklahoma County District Court in 1988. During the second trial, the state presented the same evidence as presented at the first trial: Donna Bechtel shot and killed her husband, Ken Bechtel, on the morning of September 23, 1984. Mrs. Bechtel admitted to the homicide when the police interviewed her at the residence and again at the police station on the date of the homicide. Judge Richard Freeman overruled a defense motion to dismiss at the close of the state's evidence. The attorney, representing Donna, called her as a witness to tell the jury what happened on the morning of the shooting. Donna testified that Ken Bechtel was a very abusive husband who would get stone-drunk and beat her up on a weekly basis. On the date in question, Ken came home drunk and demanded that she fix him breakfast as he pulled her out of bed. Ken then assaulted her and raped her in the bedroom of their Edmond home. Donna stated that after Ken passed out following the assault, she retrieved a gun from underneath the bed and shot him as he was asleep.

The focus of the defense case was that Donna shot her husband "in self-defense" during a lull in their domestic dispute. The defense then called as an "expert witness," a licensed psychologist, Dr. Lenore Walker, to testify about the "mental condition" of Donna Bechtel on the date of the homicide. The trial judge sustained "an objection" by the district attorney, ruling that the proposed testimony of Dr. Walker was irrelevant to the case and should not be allowed to be considered by the jury.

Dr. Walker was prepared to testify that she had reviewed all the testimony from the first trial, that she had conducted an extensive forensic examination of Donna Bechtel, and that, in her professional opinion, Donna was clearly a victim of the "battered women's syndrome. By his ruling, the district court judge denied the right of the defense to present this evidence to the jury hearing the case. After the completion of the defense evidence, the parties rested their evidence.

The jury retired and began their deliberations. Several hours later, the jury returned its verdict, finding the defendant, Donna Bechtel, guilty of first-degree murder and assessing her punishment at "life imprisonment." Donna Bechtel was returned to the Mabel Bassett Correctional Center to serve the term of life imprisonment without the possibility of parole. A second appeal of Bechtel's conviction was promulgated to the Oklahoma Court of Criminal Appeals. On September 2, 1992, the Oklahoma appeals court issued its decision. The appellate court reversed Donna Bechtel's conviction again, ruling that the trial court, Judge Richard Freeman, had committed "reversible error" by denying the defense the right to present evidence related to the issue of the "battered women's syndrome." A third trial was ordered for Donna Bechtel.

After spending eight years in prison, Donna was ready to do "anything" to get out of prison. On October 23, 1992, Donna Bechtel pled guilty to the reduced charge of manslaughter and sentenced to eight years, with credit for time served. Donna Bechtel was released from prison almost immediately and enjoyed a quiet life serving as a "lay minister" to a local church in Edmond, Oklahoma.

Analysis of the Bechtel Case

The Bechtel case is unique for several reasons. First, how could two different jury panels find the defendant, Donna Bechtel, guilty of first-degree murder and assess her punishment at life imprisonment without the possibility of parole? Was the jury system flawed in both trials? The facts of the first trial indicated that the trial court did not allow the jury to consider testimony relative to whether Donna Bechtel had waived her right to remain silent under the doctrine of Miranda a. Arizona (1966).

The appellate court concluded that the trial judge had committed reversible error by failing to allow the jury to consider such evidence. In trial number two, several years later, the trial judge refused to allow the jury to consider expert witness testimony that the defendant had "diminished mental capacity" due to her being a victim of the "battered women's syndrome." The appellate court reversed the second conviction, ruling that the judge had committed reversible error a second time by not allowing the expert testimony. A third trial was ordered. Prior to the third trial, Donna Bechtel elected to plead guilty to a reduced charge in order to get released from prison after serving eight years for a crime that would be considered "self-defense" or "justifiable homicide" in many jurisdictions in the United States. Maybe the trial judge made an innocent mistake in making erroneous rulings during both of Donna Bechtel's jury trials. There is no evidence indicating that the judge acted improperly in making these decisions except for the reasons stated in the appropriate appellate decisions in each case.

Prosecutor Misconduct

One factor in the Donna Bechtel murder trials was the office that prosecuted the case. Since the case was filed in Oklahoma County Court, the prosecution of Donna Bechtel was assigned to Oklahoma County District Attorney Bob Macy. Bob Macy was considered one of the best criminal prosecutors in the United States. During the 1980s and 1990s, Macy often stated that he had placed more people on "death row" than any other prosecutor in the entire United States. The prosecution of Donna Bechtel was a prominent case which attracted a lot of media attention:

"A wealthy oil executive killed by his wife while he was asleep in his own bed." Macy refused to examine or evaluate the possibility that Donna Bechtel deserved "some leniency" based on the history of "spousal abuse" that was present in her marriage. Macy's adamant refusal to allow the defense counsel to present expert witness testimony on the subject resulted in the second trial and conviction being reversed.

In an interesting footnote to the Bechtel case, DA Bob Macy was the subject of an investigation by the FBI in Oklahoma City, Oklahoma. The governor of Oklahoma, Frank Keating, requested the investigation. Several allegations were made in court cases that Macy's office had "fabricated evidence" in many high-profile cases. The investigation of Macy's office coupled with an investigation of the Oklahoma City Police Department revealed that Macy and Joyce Gilchrist had fabricated evidence related to "hair and fiber" evidence to link a defendant to a crime scene. The FBI reported that this type of evidence was, in fact, "false science." Macy was forced to resign his position as district attorney, a position that Macy had held for more than twenty years.

(See the book *Death and Justice in Oklahoma* by Mark Fuhrman.)

THE SINGER AND THE SKIER
Colorado v. Claudine Longet (1976)

Claudine Longet was born in Paris, France, in 1942. Claudine aspired to be an entertainer and migrated to America in 1960. Sensing that Las Vegas offered her the best chance to advance her career, Claudine moved to Las Vegas and got a job as a dancer in a show at the Tropicana Casino. Leaving the casino after a show one day, she discovered that her car had "a flat tire." Claudine was stopped along the road trying to figure out the process of how to change the flat tire. Driving down the street, entertainer Andy Williams came up on Claudine stranded at the side of the road. Andy stopped his car and helped the attractive young "damsel in distress." After taking care of her car, Andy invited her out to have dinner with him. Andy and Claudine started dating. Within a year, the pair was married. Andy Williams landed a weekly musical variety show on the 1VBC television network in 1962.

During their marriage, the couple had three children. Claudine and the kids regularly appeared on his show during its run on NBC (1962–1971). Claudine also advanced her career as an actress, appearing several television shows during the 1960s, including *Combat*, *McHale's Navy*, *1200 O'clock High*, and *The Rat Patrol*. In each of these roles, she played a young French girl, helping the US military during WWII. Claudine's singing talents exhibited on the *Andy Williams* show allowed her to land a recording contract with Herb Alpert and his company, A&M Records. Claudine recorded several hit songs that were very popular during the 1960s including "Meditation," "A Felicidade," "How Insensitive," and "We Have Only Just Begun." Many of her songs landed on most popular hits lists in the 1960s and early 1970s. Sadly, Andy Williams show was cancelled by NBC in 1971, and Claudine's singing career seem to falter. The couple separated in the early 1970s, and their divorce was finalized in 1975.

Vladimir "Spider" Sabich was born in Sacramento, California, in 1945. The Sabich family lived about fifteen miles from a prominent California ski resort, the Edelweiss Ski Resort, in the heart of the Sierra mountains in Northern California. Spider learned to ski at an early age, joining the junior skiing team at El Dorado High School. After graduation, Spider was offered a college scholarship to the University of Colorado in Boulder, Colorado. His college coach in Colorado turned out to be Bob Beattie, the captain of the US ski team that was preparing for the 1968 Winter Olympics. Spider was recruited to participate in the Olympics. Spider won a World Cup victory at South Lake Tahoe and was crowned the Downhill champion during the 1968 season. Spider won more national acclaim in the late 1960s and early 1970s. Spider's fame inspired a movie starring Robert Bedford entitled *Downhill Racer*! While the prize money for winning a skiing championship was modest, Spider's popularity allowed him to do make numerous television advertisements, netting more than $250,000 per year. The additional income allowed Spider to build a chalet-style house in the resort area outside of Aspen, Colorado. In early 1975, Spider suffered a serious injury to his knee, and he was forced to sit out the ski seasons in 1975 and 1976. Spider met Claudine Longet at a procelebrity event in Bear Valley, California, in the early 1970s. The pair struck up a great friendship and started dating in 1974. With her marriage to Andy Williams "on the rocks," Claudine decided to move to Aspen to be near Spider as they relationship became very close. After her divorce was finalized in 1975, Claudine and Spider decided to live together. Claudine moved with her three children into Spider's big chalet mansion. For several months, the relationship appeared to a union made "in heaven." That all changed on the afternoon of March 21, 1976. Spider was shot and killed at his home. Subsequently, Claudine Longet was arrested and charged with first-degree murder in the district court of Colorado!

The Police Investigation

On March 21, 1976, around 5:30 p.m., Claudine Longet rushed to the telephone to call 911. Her dear boyfriend, Spider Sabich, had just been shot. An ambulance was dispatched to the house to take Spider to the hospital. Claudine accompanied him.

The paramedics rendered emergency aid to the skier. Spider died before the ambulance could reach the hospital emergency room. Officers with the Aspen Police Department met with Claudine at the hospital and interviewed her about the circumstances leading up to the shooting. Claudine told the police that it was "an accident"! Claudine stated "that the gun went off by accident as Spider was showing it to me!" The police took custody of the gun, a .22-caliber pistol, and placed it into a plastic evidence bag. The gun was subsequently forwarded to the state crime lab for a forensic examination of the possible murder weapon.

The gun used in the shooting turned out to be "a Luger WWII model pistol" that Spider's father had given him several years earlier. The police conducted an extensive search of the house and confiscated several items from the chalet including Claudine's diary. Claudine was arrested later that evening and charged with the crime of first-degree murder. The crime of murder in Colorado carries a possible punishment of life imprisonment. After being booked into the county jail, Claudine was permitted one phone call, to a family friend.

Her friend subsequently contacted Andy Williams in Los Angeles, California. The following day, March 22, 1976, Andy flew up to Aspen and visited with Claudine at the local jail. Andy assured Claudine that he would take care of their children and that everything would be okay. In the next few days, Andy checked around town to locate the best criminal defense attorney in the Colorado. Ron Austin of Aspen was hired to represent Claudine in the murder case.

Colorado v. Claudine Longet

On the evening of the shooting, a police officer from the Aspen Police Department responded to the shooting. Entering the residence with a private security guard, the officer assisted emergency person-nel in getting Sabich loaded into an ambulance to be transported to the hospital. The officer allowed Claudine to leave the crime scene and accompany the victim to the hospital. The officer remained at the chalet and made a thorough search of the large chalet belonging to Sabich. During the search of the house, the officer found the mur-der weapon, a .22-caliber pistol, and placed it in an evidence bag. A further search uncovered Claudine's diary in the master bedroom. The diary contained notes related to the "ongoing domestic dispute" between the victim and Claudine. One entry in the diary indicated that Spider wanted Claudine to move out of the house by the end of the month (March 31, 1976). After completing his search, the officer took several photographs of the interior of the house and the crime scene. Completing his search, the officer contacted a second Aspen police officer who was standing by at the hospital. The police decided to take Claudine to the police station for further questioning about the circumstances surrounding the shooting. The Aspen police requested that a nurse at the hospital take "a blood sample" from Claudine before leaving the hospital. Claudine objected to being forced to give the blood sample. Upon orders from the Aspen police, the nurse took the sample, anyway. After the procedure was completed, Claudine was taken to the Aspen police station for further questioning. Prior to the interrogation, Claudine was advised of her rights under the Miranda warnings. Claudine invoked her Miranda rights and would not answer any questions. Claudine was arrested and placed in jail.

A couple of days later, Claudine was charged in the death of the Olympic skier, Spider Sabich. Claudine, represented by local attor-ney Ron Austin, entered a plea of "*not guilty*" and requested a jury trial. The request was granted, and the case was set for trial several months later. During the period of time leading up to the trial, her defense counsel, Ron Austin, filed several motions related to the cir-cumstances leading up to her arrest. A discovery request demanded copies of all reports and items of evidence that would be used at the trial of the case. In addition, a motion to suppress certain items from being used as evidence in court. The items that were included in the motion to suppress included the gun taken from the house, the diary belonging to Claudine, and the blood sample that Claudine were forced to give at the hospital prior to her arrest.

At an evidentiary hearing on the motions, the trial judge sustained the motion to suppress and prohibited the state of Colorado from using or mentioning the evidence during the trial of the case. The state of Colorado appealed this ruling to the Supreme Court of Colorado, claiming that the trial judge had committed "reversible error" by denying the state to present this important evidence to the jury. The Colorado Supreme Court denied the state's appeal in 1976 and ordered the trial to proceed. The suppression of this evidence severely hampered the state at the trial!

At the trial of the case in January, 1977, the state presented testimony from the police officers at the crime scene about the condition of the victim and the discovery of the murder weapon. A representative of the coroner's office testified about the results of the autopsy: that Spider Sabich had died as the result of a gunshot wound to the stomach.

Expert testimony elicited by the state's witnesses indicated that the gun had been fired from more than six feet away from the victim since there was no gunpowder residue on the body on the victim. Additional testimony indicated that the point of entry for the fatal shot was in the back of the victim, supporting the theory that he was facing away from Claudine when the fatal shot was fired. A forensic expert identified the gun, a German Luger, as being the murder weapon. The gun was identified as belonging to Steve Sabich, the brother of the Spider Sabich. Apparently, Steve Sabich had asked his brother to store the gun in a closet at the large chalet house that Spider lived in. The gun was placed in a closet near the master bedroom of the house by Spider himself. The state rested its case. The trial judge overruled an oral motion to dismiss the case due to insufficient evidence.

The Defense of Claudine Longet

The attorneys for Claudine Longet called a "firearms expert" to testify about the weapon used to kill Spider. The witness, considered a gun expert, testified that the gun was clearly "defective": that the firing mechanism on the gun was defective and that the gun could accidently discharge a bullet without the trigger on the gun being pulled. The defense attorney, Ron Austin, called Claudine to the witness stand. Claudine testified that she found the gun in closet and that she took the gun out when Spider came home. Claudine asked Spider about the gun and the idea of whether the gun should even be in the house since she had her children staying with them. Spider assured her that the gun was defective and that the gun could not be fired. Suddenly, the gun went off. *Bam!*

Claudine dropped the gun and ran over to Spider as he slumped against the wall and fell onto the floor. Spider was bleeding profusely. Within a few seconds, Spider slipped into unconsciousness. Claudine immediately called 911 to get medical attention for Spider. Claudine traveled with Spider in the ambulance, rushing him to an Aspen hospital. Claudine testified that the shooting was a "tragic accident" and that she felt "lost" without him.

The Jury Verdict

The trial testimony lasted four full days. At the conclusion of the evidence, Judge Lohr recessed the trial and summoned the attorneys to his chambers to review the court's instructions that should be given to the jury. The state's attorney argued that the proper charge was "murder" and that the defendant should be sentenced to a term of life imprisonment. The defense counsel argued that the case was one of involuntary manslaughter or negligent homicide. Judge Lohr elected to give the jury instructions covering the various charges that the jury could consider in reaching a verdict. The closing arguments were presented by the state's attorney and defense counsel, Ronald Austin. The jury retired to begin deliberations. Approximately, four hours later, the jury returned to the courtroom with the verdict: "We the jury, being duly impaneled to hear the witnesses and the evidence presented in this case, do, hereby, find the defendant, Claudine Longet, *guilty* of the crime of negligent homicide, and we recommend a punishment as a misdemeanor offense." Judge Lohr discharged the jury and set the case for judgment and sentencing on January 31, 1977.

The Sentence of the Court

On January 31, 1977, Judge Lohr conducted the sentencing hearing to consider the proper punishment for the defendant. The judge allowed the state to present evidence in the form of victim's impact statements from the family of Spider Sabich. Judge Lohr then allowed Claudine to address the court. Claudine stated the shooting was a "tragic accident." Claudine begged for the court to grant her probation so that she would not be separated from her three small children. Judge Lohr made a lengthy statement relating to his considerations in passing sentence on Claudine. The judge indicated that he had received letters from all over America, supporting Claudine and that she should be given leniency. Judge Lohr concluded that the defendant, Claudine Longet, was guilty of the crime of negligent homicide as determined by the jury. The judge then ordered the defendant be sentenced to "thirty days" in the county jail and that the defendant could serve the term on alternating weekends when the children were with their natural father, Andy Williams. The Aspen community and Spider's family were totally shocked by the leniency of the Colorado court. Claudine served the sentence over the next six months in the county jail. Claudine left the courtroom with entertainer Andy Williams, who had been present the entire trial. Outside the courtroom, the couple was joined by her three children. Spider's family was extremely upset by the outcome of the trial. A few months later, the Sabich family filed a $1.3 million wrongful-death lawsuit against Claudine Longet in the district court of Colorado. The lawsuit was settled out of court. The case file was sealed, with both sides signing a "secret agreement" never to talk about the case every again.

Analysis of the Claudine Longet Case

A prominent America athlete, an Olympic skiing champion, shot in the back inside his own home. The shooter, a well-known singer and Hollywood entertainer! Was the killing of Spider Sabich a cold-blooded murder or a tragic accident? How could the shooter, Claudine Longet, walk away after only serving thirty days in a Colorado jail? Was justice served? Did a public celebrity use money and fame to get away with what some people would consider "cold-blood murder"? Does money and fame buy "justice in America"? There are a lot of unanswered questions posed by the Claudine Longet case. The suppression of "key evidence" in the case may have influenced the jury to recommend leniency to the court in assessing proper punishment in the case. Claudine has not spoken publicly about the case in more than forty years. Claudine has lived a very private life in Aspen with her current husband, her defense attorney, Ron Austin!

TWO BIRDS WITH ONE BLAST
Texas v. Tracy Roberson (2007)

Tracy Roberson was born in the Fort Worth, Texas, area in 1970s. Tracy attended the public system in the Fort Worth area. While in high school, Tracy met Darrell Roberson, who was a couple of years older than her. Tracy and Darrell started dating, attending local football and basketball games. After the games, they would go out and enjoy pizza.

Darrell was a graduating senior who wanted to get a good-paying job in the real estate business. Soon after graduation, Darrell prepared to take the Texas state licensing exam to become a licensed realtor. Darrell passed the Texas State Licensing Exam and got his real estate license. Darrell became established as a real estate broker. Darrell, feeling secure in his job, proposed to Tracy, asking her to marry him. Tracy accepted his proposal, and the couple got married in 1990. A few years later, Tracy had the couple first child, a daughter they named Kyla. Since Darrell was successful in the real estate business, this permitted Tracy to be a "stay-at-home mom," taking care of their daughter. A couple of years later, Tracy gave birth to a second beautiful young girl they named Julie. In 2000, Tracy gave birth to a third baby, another adorable baby girl. Tracy enjoyed being a "stay-at-home mom" to her three beautiful little girls. From all appearances, the Roberson family was the typical all-American family. Darrell was a very successful real estate broker, and Tracy was the perfect mother to their little girls. Appearances can be deceiving! Behind the scenes, there was hidden turbulence in the form of "domestic strife and spousal abuse." Darrell was the breadwinner and controlled the family's finances. Darrell's attitude was that he would "call all the shots" in the marriage and that Tracy would have to do exactly as he said. If Tracy failed to follow orders, Darrell would lash out and give her "a whipping"! Darrell would slap her, punch her, and beat her into submission.

Tracy got more depressed with each passing year in her marriage. Darrell was very controlling and demanding. The only thing that kept Tracy going was taking care of her three adorable girls. Tracy felt like she was trapped in hopeless situation! That there was no escape from Darrell's jail.

The only time that Tracy got to herself was while Darrell was busy at his real estate office and the girls were at school. Tracy considered a separation and a possible divorce. Darrell's response: "No way!" Every time that she tried to leave, Darrell would assault her and beat her into submission. Her dreary life changed in the summer of 2006. As a part of her weekly routine, Tracy would go to the Walmart to shop for groceries and other household necessities which the girls needed.

One afternoon, she met Devin LaSalle, a very polite younger man with a warm friendly smile. During one conversation, Tracy learned that Devin worked at the UPS terminal at the Dallas-Fort Worth airport. Later, Tracy ran into Devin at Eisenhower Middle School where both of their children attended. After a few weeks of friendly conversations, Devin and Tracy exchanged phone numbers and started talking and texting back and forth on a daily basis. Tracy told Devin that she was unhappy in her marriage. They agreed to meet a convenient place and enjoy some "adult privacy" for a few hours. Tracy was amazed at the pleasure she experienced while she was with Devin. Their relationship got more intense during the fall of 2006. One evening, Tracy texted Devin, advising him that she wanted to see him. Devin texted her back, stating that he would stop by her house at midnight.

That evening, Darrell was playing cards with his real estate buddies in Dallas and would be gone most of the night. When Devin arrived at the house, he parked in Tracy's driveway and called her. Tracy, after taking the house phone off the hook, walked out and got in Devin's truck. Tracy was only wearing a pair of panties and silk robe. After a few minutes of pleasant conversation, Tracy opened her robe and invited Devin to take care of her.

Murder in the Morning (December 11, 2006)

Darrell was playing cards with his real estate friends on the evening of December 10, 2006. Picking up his cellphone, he called Tracy at home, to tell her that the poker game was winding down and that he was coming home. Getting a busy signal, Darrell wondered whom would Tracy be talking to this time of night. After playing a final hand, Darrell called his house four times in the next few minutes. Each time, Darrell got a busy signal. Darrell got in his car and started racing home. Calling three more times, Darrell got a "busy signal" each time. Darrell was very concerned! Were Tracy and the girls okay? Entering the neighborhood, Darrell turned onto his street and put his headlights on bright. Nearing his house, Darrell could see that there was a strange-looking blue Chevrolet pickup in his driveway. Who was there? A friend of Tracy's? What was going on? Darrell sensed trouble. Slowly down, Darrell pulled over to the side of the street and turned off the motor. Darrell heard the voice of a woman, Tracy. She was screaming, "Oh my God! Help, please help me!" Reacting quickly, Darrell reached into the center console of his Ford SUV and pulled out his weapon, a .38-caliber pistol. Jumping out of his truck, Darrell approached the truck. All of a sudden, Darrell observed the truck start up, back down into the street, and start to speed away. Unsure what was going on, Darrell raised his pistol and started shooting. *Bam! Bam! Bam! Bam!* The first three shots missed the target. Darrell observed a person jumping out onto the street and landing in the neighbor's front yard!

The final shot pierced the back window of the truck, apparently hitting the driver of the pickup! The truck veered off the street and crashed into a tree located in nearby neighbors' yard! The truck burst into flames caught on fire. What had just happened? Who was in the truck? Who jumped out of the truck and landed in a nearby yard? Darrell ran up to the scene to see!

The Police Investigation

Upon hearing the crash of the pickup truck into a tree in his yard, a neighbor called 911 to summon police and fire units. Two patrol officers responded within fifteen minutes. A firetruck was summoned to the scene to assist in putting out the truck fire. Darrell was placed in a police car and questioned about what had just happened there. Darrell told the police that he saw the blue Chevy truck in his driveway. Darrell's first thought: Tracy was seeing another man! After hearing the screams of a woman, Darrell was shocked! Darrell retrieved his gun and started firing at the truck as it attempted to leave the area.

Darrell acknowledged that he fired a total of four shots at the fleeing blue pickup truck. After the last shot, Darrell observed the truck veer off the street and hit a nearby tree. Darrell ran down the street to determine who the person was who jumped out of the truck as it was fleeing the crime scene. Darrell was shocked when he got there and saw his wife, Tracy, lying on the grass. Darrell grabbed Tracy up and dragged her back to the house. Once the truck fire was put out, firemen removed the body of Devin LaSalle from the truck. The remains were examined and taken to the Tarrant County coroner's office for an autopsy. After approximately ninety minutes, Darrell was arrested and taken to the Tarrant County Jail for booking. The charge: first-degree murder!

Tracy Roberson was placed in a separate police car and questioned about what had just happened at her residence. Tracy stated that Devin LaSalle was a friend who stopped by the house after getting off work that evening. Tracy stated that she got in Devin's truck to talk for a few minutes. That during their conversation, Darrell showed up and pulled out his gun and started shooting. Deville started his truck and backed out of the driveway, trying to get away. Tracy jumped out of the truck and collapsed on the ground as Devin was trying to get away!

The Grand Jury Investigation

During the next three months, law enforcement completed their investigation into the homicide that resulted in the death of Devin LaSalle. The autopsy report along with forensic evidence was submitted for the Tarrant County grand jury to consider.

The sworn testimony of Darrell Roberson and Tracy Roberson were also presented to the grand jury. After receiving all the applicable evidence gathered by the local law enforcement, the grand jury retired to begin their deliberations on what types of charges should be filed in the case. On March 30, 2007, the Tarrant County returned with their findings. The grand jury issued a criminal indictment, charging the person responsible for the death of Devin LaSalle, to wit, Tracy Roberson was charged with the crime of manslaughter! An arrest warrant was issued for Tracy Roberson. A few days later, Tracy Roberson was arraigned in the district court of Tarrant County, Texas, on the charge of "second-degree manslaughter." Tracy entered a plea of "*not guilty*" and requested a trial by a jury. Tracy selected Jill Davis to represent her in the manslaughter charges that had filed against her. The criminal case slowly moved through the criminal justice process in Tarrant County. The case finally was set for a jury trial in May 2008. During the trial, the state presented evidence indicating that the death of Devin LaSalle was caused by solely by the actions of Tracy Roberson. The state's case was predicated on the idea that Darrell only shot and killed Devin LaSalle after perceiving that Devin LaSalle was assaulting and raping his wife in the driveway of their home. Tracy had, upon seeing Darrell approaching the house, started yelling, "Help, I am being raped." Darrell then shot and killed Devin LaSalle!

The Defense of Tracy Roberson

The defense attorney for Tracy Roberson, Jill Davis, called several witnesses on behalf of the defense. Tracy's cousin testified that she would visit with Tracy at least once or twice each month.

The cousin stated that she observed Tracy as having "bumps and bruises" on her face, arms, and legs when they would go out to lunch together. The relative described Tracy's marriage as an "abusive relationship" that had gone on for almost twenty years. She could not understand why Tracy stayed married to Darrell. Another relative described in great detail the abuse that Tracy had suffered at the hands of Darrell during their marriage. The witness described an incident in particular when Darrell pulled a gun out of the closet and threatened to kill Tracy if she ever attempted to leave him. She described Tracy as an "abused wife" who was terrorized by Darrell and his constant threats toward her. Tracy took the witness stand and testified in her own defense. Tracy testified that Darrell was her "high school sweetheart" and that Darrell was the only man that she had ever known for her almost twenty years of marriage. Tracy described her friendship with Devin LaSalle. That they met at Walmart and talked, eventually exchanging phone numbers. Tracy testified that she had meet privately with Devin on a few occasions. Tracy admitted that she invited Devin over to her house on the evening of December 10, 2006, and that Darrell got there about midnight and that she went out to talk with him for a few minutes. Getting in his truck, Tracy noticed, almost immediately, that Devin was intoxicated. His breath smelled of alcohol! Tracy stated that Devin became very aggressive, trying to rip her clothes off. Tracy stated that as they were struggling, Darrell drove up to the house.

Tracy yelled, "Oh my God!" Devin started the truck and started backing out of the driveway. Getting into the street, Devin started racing away. When the first shot rang out, Tracy testified that she ducked down on the floorboard of the truck to avoid being hit by the flying bullets!

Tracy stated that she feared that she was going to be shot by Darrell if she didn't jump out of the truck. Opening the door, Tracy leaped out of the truck and landed in the front yard of a neighbor's house. Tracy stated that she looked up, just in time, to see Devin's truck veer off the street, striking a large tree! Tracy stated that she saw the truck explode into flames immediately. Tracy collapsed on the ground! A few seconds later, Darrell dragged her into the house. Tracy finished her testimony and was excused from the witness stand. The judge recessed the trial and told the attorneys to meet with him in the judge's chambers. During the closed-door meeting, the judge reviewed the evidence and advised the attorneys that he was going to give the jury instructions on the evidence that had been presented and the possible verdicts that the jury could render in the case. After closing arguments by the attorneys for the state and the defense, the judge advised the jury to retire and deliberate.

The Jury Verdict

The jury deliberated for several hours with no verdict. Why was the jury unable to agree on a possible verdict? Would there be a mistrial and a retrial of the case before a different jury?

On the second day of jury deliberations, the jury returned with a verdict. The judge reviewed the verdict and advised Tracy to stand and face the jury. The judge read the verdict: "We, the jury sworn to hear the evidence and decide the verdict, finds as follows: we find the defendant, Tracy Roberson, '*guilty* of the crime of *manslaughter*' and fix her punishment at *five years* in prison." Tracy collapsed into her chair as the judge excused the jury. The following week, Tracy was formally sentenced by the judge to serve a term of *five years* in prison in the killing of Devin LaSalle!

Analysis of the Tracy Roberson Case

The Tracy Roberson case is one of the most unique cases in the history of the American criminal justice system. The facts of the homicide that resulted in the death of Devin LaSalle are undisputed. Darrell Roberson shot and killed Devin LaSalle in the early morning hours of December 11, 2006. While Darrell was arrested and held on a charge of murder, a grand jury indicted his wife on a charge of manslaughter. Darrell was never officially charged with a crime. Tracy was ultimately convicted and sentenced to serve a term of five years in the Texas State Prison for Women. How could this happen? There are several factors to consider. These factors include the following:

1. Darrell was only acting to protect his wife and family when he shot and killed Devin LaSalle, who was fleeing from the crime scene. That was the prosecutor's contention in pushing for the conviction of Tracy Roberson. In retrospect, what crime had Devin LaSalle committed? If it

was a consensual act that Devin was engaged in with Tracy
Roberson, then there was no crime and no justification for
the shooting.

2.   Tracy was engaged in an immoral act of committing "adul-
tery" when she engaged in a sexual relationship with Devin
LaSalle. The jury obviously based its decision on the issue
of "immorality" rather than standard legal principles.

3.   The jury and the court totally ignored the defense of Tracy
Roberson that she was a victim of "the battered women's
syndrome," after enduring twenty years of physical and
mental abuse at the hands of Darrell Roberson.

The Tracy Roberson case is truly a "miscarriage of justice" that
should never been allowed to happen in American criminal justice
system. Texas justice seems to be totally different from any other state
in the United States.

FINAL ANALYSIS
Women Who Kill

Analysis of the Twenty Homicide Cases
Where the Woman Kills a Man

A review of the above cases reveals that in 50 percent of the cases (ten out of the twenty), the woman was found "not guilty" of the homicide charges filed against her. With regard to the remaining ten cases, only three of the women were sentenced to serve a term in excess of one year in jail. Seven of the ten women received sentences of less than ninety days in jail. The obvious question presented in reviewing these cases is *why*? Does a woman receive more "lenient treatment" in the American criminal justice system than a man does?

Factors to Be Considered in Homicide
Cases Where the Killer Is a Woman

1. *Women on the jury*: Women serving as jurors in a murder case where a woman is charged with the murder of a man may offer "a woman's prospective" on matters related to domestic relations disputes. A woman juror may possess "sympathy" for a woman who is forced to endure an abusive spouse.

2. *Prosecutor misconduct*: State prosecutors in many of the cases under review failed to consider "mitigating evidence" such as spousal abuse in filing felony charges against the woman. Many of the women were charged with first-degree murder instead of a lesser included offense such as manslaughter.

The jury, the trial judge, and in some cases the appellate court had to step in and overrule the actions of the prosecuting authority in seeking excessive punishment against the woman. (See the case of *Oklahoma v. Donna Bechtel 1984*).

3. *Self-defense*: Any person has the right of "self-defense" if they are in their home or any other place where they have a legal right to be. The right of "self-dense" allows any person to use deadly force if they are in "imminent danger" of being seriously injured or killed by any person. See the cases of *Alabama v. Dixon (2018)* and *Virginia v. Susan Cummings (1997)*.

4. "*The battered woman's syndrome defense*": In the last thirty years, the American legal system has allowed the use of the "battered women's syndrome" if there is credible evidence presented by the defense to justify the trial court to present instructions to the jury on the issue of the accused being a "battered woman." The defense must present the following evidences:

   a. multiple instances of continuing physical and mental abuse by the homicide victim prior to the date of the homicide,

   b. a history of prior complaints to the local police and law enforcement relative to the woman being abused by the man,

   c. multiple medical records showing that the woman has sustained physical injuries that required medical attention at local doctors and hospitals, and

   d. expert testimony from a licensed mental health professional indicated that the woman is an example of being "a battered woman."

The courts in more than twenty states now recognize the concept of the "battered woman's syndrome" being a viable defense in any homicide where a woman is charged with killing the man.

In all homicide case involving a woman accused of murder, law enforcement authorities, prosecutors, and defense attorneys should analyze the growing trend in the American legal system that allows a woman to present "mitigating evidence" when the woman employs "deadly force" to protect herself from physical harm or extract herself from an "abusive relationship" with a husband or boyfriend.

BIBLIOGRAPHY

1. Sara Marino, "Martin County Newspaper," November 26, 2018.
2. Nolan Clay, "Daily Oklahoman" April 12, 1986.
3. Donna Bechtel v. State of Oklahoma, 738 P. 2nd, 559, (1987).
4. Jennifer Ordonez, Washington Post Newspaper, May 21, 1998.
5. Nickie Mayo, Independence Mail Newspaper, August 2, 2017.
6. Laura Morel, Tampa Bay Times newspaper, May 12, 2017.
7. Michael Cohen, Tampa Bay Times newspaper, March 22, 2017.
8. Peter Van Zant, CBS NEWS "48 Hours" October 15, 2016.
9. Associated Press, May 15, 2016.
10. Eddie Dean, Washington Post Newspaper, October 31, 1997.
11. Brooke Masters, Washington Post Newspaper, May 14, 1998.
12. Rachel Rice, St. Louis Post-Dispatch, January 22, 2019.
13. JJ Duncan, "Krazy Killers" June 30, 2014.
14. Associated Press, May 8, 2008.
15. Melissa Jeltson, The Huffington Post, March 21, 2016.
16. Fort Bend County News, February 22, 2011.
17. Bill Barr, Tulsa World Newspaper, February 20, 2000.
18. Jane Harper, The Virginia Beach News, December 5, 2018.
19. Tracy Roberson Interview, Fort Worth Star Telegram, March 31, 2007.
20. www.KWTX.news.com. March 31, 2007.
21. Court Opinion, Texas Court of Appeals, 2nd District, August 5, 2010.
22. "Burning Bed," www.cbc.news.com, 1977.
23. "Burning Bed," The Movie, Farrah Fawcett, 1981.

ABOUT THE AUTHOR

Dan Brown is a well-known professional in the field of criminal justice, having served as a police officer, prosecutor, and defense counsel, handling more than five hundred felony cases in the past forty years. More recently, Dan has served as a professor of criminal justice and political science at Southwestern Oklahoma State University. Professor Brown's previous published books include *Critical Issues in Criminal Justice* and, most recently, *Crime Victim*.

Printed by BoD™in Norderstedt, Germany